Praise for *Five Pillars of Pro*

"*Five Pillars of Prosperity* is an excellent resource for people of all faiths. I strongly believe this book will be life changing for all readers, as it will help them to understand the basics of finance, Islamic finance, and financial responsibility, leading to a more fulfilling and prosperous life spiritually and financially."

> –Imam Mohamed Maged, Executive Director, Religious Affairs, ADAMS Center, and President, Islamic Society of North America

"*Five Pillars of Prosperity* provides great advice on the value of solid, basic principles that can and should guide us in life, in our family, or in our business. It is good advice whether you are Christian, Muslim, or Jewish. Yaqub Mirza has put a lot of wisdom between the covers of this book."

> –John H. Sununu, former Governor of New Hampshire and White House Chief of Staff under President George H. W. Bush

"I loved this book! Not only does Dr. Mirza educate the reader as to the principles of Islamic investing, he illuminates the guiding principles of a religion many of us know only through the cloudy lens of recent and devastating historical events. Because he has made accessible to his readers these principles—principles which are the essence of all religions—he has undertaken a tremendous public service, one too few of our educators have the ability to undertake. Too little time has been spent and attention paid to making all of us understand that 'we are in this together.' Dr. Mirza is to be admired for doing so effectively and in a manner guaranteed to leave the reader wiser."

> –Nancy Luque, Principal Attorney and Partner, Luque Marino LLP

"At a time when too often it seems the only moral instruction provided by Wall Street is 'go forth and mulitply,' Yaqub Mirza offers an enriching alternative. It is easily read, but even my mentor, Sir John Templeton, the 'dean of global investing,' would have appreciated it. Though a

Christian in the mold of John Calvin, Sir John also avoided the debt, speculation, and other potentially harmful activities that Dr. Mirza explains are to be avoided according to Shariah law. It should reassure our increasingly financialized world that the three great Abrahamic faiths are as relevant as ever and offer the world far more unified solutions for peace and prosperity than the nightly news often implies."

–Gary Moore, author of *Faithful Finances 101*

"Yaqub Mirza provides readers with advice about personal financial habits and planning that is very important and useful for people of all faiths. His main contribution lies in showing that this advice can be made consistent with Islamic finance principles by only small modifications in behavior and choice of financial strategies. His work fills an important and much-neglected niche in the market for financial planning advice."

–Herbert Grubel, Professor of Economics Emeritus, Simon Fraser University, and Senior Fellow, the Fraser Institute, Canada

"*Five Pillars of Prosperity* is a beautiful piece of writing that reflects what this Christian has learned about Islamic values. I particularly admire the emphasis on the acceptability of generating wealth and, after meeting reasonable family needs, recycling the surplus for the benefit of community and society. This includes all religious traditions and those who profess no particular faith. The Hebrew prophets and Jesus agree."

–Joseph V. Montville, Chair of Center for World Religions, Diplomacy, and Conflict Resolution, George Mason University

"*Five Pillars of Prosperity* is a rare interfaith work of how to apply religion and philosophy in everyday life. It confirms what I have long believed: wealth and possessions are worthless in themselves. Their only proper purpose is to aid in doing God's will—which is the only truly lasting thing a person will ever do. Possessions will possess their owner until he or she realizes that they are not an end but a means to an end—a tool, not a goal—and that in any event, possessions are ours

only for a short time. *Five Pillars* offers good, solid advice on how to live those convictions."
–Lewis Perdue, entrepreneur and *New York Times* best-selling author

"Dr. Mirza offers practical insight into personal finance and investment that is both useful and easy to follow for Muslims and non-Muslims alike. It should be a help to savers and investors at all levels."
–Sandra Spalletta, Manager and General Counsel,
BW Realty Advisors LLC

"It is best to learn from those who have actually practiced what it is they are teaching. There is no finer representative of the principles in this book than Dr. Mirza. His life is a testament to the principles laid out within these pages. If you want to achieve economic well-being and spiritual fulfillment, read this book."
–Dr. Miles K. Davis, Dean of Harry F. Byrd
School of Business, Shenandoah University

"It is widely assumed that Shari'ah-compliant investing is not consistent with Wall Street finance. In *Five Pillars of Prosperity*, Dr. Yaqub Mirza, an expert in both approaches to finance, demonstrates that this is not the case and shows the reader how modern financial transactions can satisfy the demands of major western commercial markets while remaining Shari'ah-compliant. It is a welcome contribution to the increasingly complex international world of modern finance."
–Richard Gross, Attorney and Senior Manager, BW Realty Advisors

"When I think of your treatise on investing, only one word comes to mind: *terrific*. I was especially taken with the way you integrated wisdom for daily living with your investment advice. I must say, I had to chuckle when I read your definition of passion, i.e., 'If you love what you do, you will never work a day in your life.' It occurred to me that this is the enviable state in which I have found myself for at least 85 percent of my life, after holding numerous jobs in a number of different career fields. Yes, I

have been blessed, just as your book will be a blessing to all who read it."
–Dr. Douglas M. Johnston, President and Founder, International
Center for Religion and Diplomacy; author, *Religion, Terror, and Error*

"The book provides invaluable advice on a holistic approach to wealth creation that will be of universal appeal. There is substance and spirit, theory and practice that readers will find useful in their quest for a harmonious balance in pursuing the good life."
–Anwar Ibrahim, Former Deputy Prime Minister
and Finance Minister, and Member of Parliament, Malaysia

"In a culture where greed and wealth building is rooted in living beyond your means, and where financial institutions own everything you use or have, Dr. Mirza shows us a path to achieve prosperity and acquire wealth while living within our means, debt free! It is impressive that he bases his plan on a lifestyle of morality and adherence to one's faith. He surprises the reader with the relevance of Shari'ah to achieving the 'American Dream' in our pursuit of happiness—a timely endeavor while the scare of 'Shari'ah' is propagated by bigotry, ignorance, and hate."
–Dr. Jamal Barzinji, President, International
Institute of Islamic Thought, USA

"What I appreciate most about Dr. Mirza in his teaching work, and now in his book, is the way he makes 'wealth building' a relevant topic to even those with limited means and limited understanding about the world of finances. Using his own personal experiences and other very practical examples, readers can develop a positive, intentional, and faith-inspired relationship with money."
–Salma Elkadi Abugideiri, Professional Counselor

"One of the greatest contributions a person can make is to facilitate the acquisition of awareness, knowledge, and skills to support the practice of one's faith—this is precisely what Dr. Mirza has accomplished in *Five Pillars to Prosperity*. Although in theory all of us are familiar with the principles of earning, saving, investing, spending, and giving, Muslims and other faith-inspired people will benefit tremendously from the unselfish manner in which the author shares from his personal and professional experiences with living out these principles. At a time of such current economic uncertainty, Dr. Mirza's book will certainly provide much practical relief and advice to the reader on how to go about as an informed participant in the process of faith-based wealth building."

–Altaf Husain, Assistant Professor, Howard University

"Dr Mirza has now put on paper how he has lived and raised his children to be wise and to pass this knowledge to future generations. Financial responsibility should be passed along to our family and this book will help all who read it in that task. 'Train up a child in the way he should go and when he is old he will not depart from it' (Proverbs 22:6)."
Doug Carnes, Pastor, and Board Member, Mar-Jac Poultry

"Dr. Mirza's book teaches a way of conducting business based on Muslim principles. This was something really new for me, and I am sure it is for many people educated in Western society regardless of their religious affiliation. Maybe from time to time someone speaks or writes about good behavior in doing business and being charitable, but practicing it in the way he describes in his book seems rare. This makes an important difference, which is well illustrated with examples from his own experience."

–Sergio Araya, General Manager, Sterling Agricola S.A.

Five Pillars *of* Prosperity

Essentials of Faith-Based Wealth Building

M. YAQUB MIRZA

WHITE CLOUD PRESS
ASHLAND, OREGON

White Cloud Press books may be purchased for educational, business, or sales
promotional use. For information, please write: Special Market Department,
White Cloud Press, PO Box 3400, Ashland, OR 97520
Website: www.whitecloudpress.com

Illustrations by Alaa Fadag
Cover and Interior Design by C Book Services

First edition: 2014

Printed in the United States of America

Library of Congress Cataloging-in-Publication Data

Mirza, M. Yaqub.
Five pillars of prosperity : essentials of faith-based wealth building / M. Yaqub
Mirza.
pages cm
Includes bibliographical references and index.
ISBN 978-1-935952-88-6 (pbk.)
1. Finance, Personal. 2. Success in business. 3. Investments. I. Title.
HG179.M5267 2014
332.024'01--dc23
2013042677

MIX
Paper from
responsible sources
FSC
www.fsc.org   FSC® C011935

To my parents, siblings (especially Dr. Ishaq Mirza), in-laws, children, extended family, and my beloved wife, Tanveer
also
to my brothers and sisters in Abrahamic faith
and all other faiths who desire to live in peace, love, and prosperity

General Disclaimer

The information contained in this book was obtained from various sources. The author does not guarantee its accuracy or completeness nor the accuracy or completeness of the analysis relating to it. Any party relying on the contents will be doing so at his or her own discretion.

This book is for general circulation and is provided for general information only. It should be treated as a guide and as a service to community. The information, examples, and case studies in this book are intended to be a general introduction to financial management. They are not intended to be either a specific offer by any Sterling Management Group Inc. entity or person to sell or provide, or a specific invitation to apply for, any particular product or service. Sterling Management Group Inc. and its affiliates offer a broad range of investment advisory and financial services. The nature and degree of advice and assistance provided, the fees charged, and client rights and Sterling Management Group Inc.'s obligations will differ among these services. Neither Sterling Management Group Inc. nor its personnel provide individual legal or tax advice. Clients should review any planned financial transactions and strategies that may have legal or tax implications with their personal advisors.

Although the author is a founder and trustee of Amana Mutual Funds Trust and a board member of University Islamic Financial (UIF), a subsidiary of the University Bank, the work is entirely that of the author. Neither the Trust nor its advisor, Saturna Capital Corporation, nor UIF and University Bank, suggested the creation or production of this work.

Contents

Foreword

Prosperity has long been cherished as a goal. The desire is universal and rightly so. Prosperity is desired to provide an atmosphere congenial for living in peace, with dignity. Human beings are here on earth to demonstrate that one can be good by choice. They are to compete with one another in attaining moral excellence. That is what raised humans' stature not only above animals but also above angels, the "no sin, no wrong-doing" creatures!

In the hundred fifty or so pages that follow these lines, Dr. Mirza, whom I have known as pious people's money manager since 1972, when we first met, tells you how to go about working for prosperity. The message is simple: earn, save, invest, spend, and give. What is unique about it that justifies writing a book? Well, for a complete answer you have to read the book. But I can tell you something to begin with. The significance lies in the sequence. Also, each one of these five steps implies a certain mindset, rather, an ethic. Focus on these and you have your answer.

Earning requires working, which calls for some self-discipline, and that brings in the big question of motivation. History is witness to the interesting relationship between strength and weakness of motivation and the rise and fall of civilizations, Islamic civilization being no exception. The Prophet (peace be upon him) had some strongly motivated people around him. Motivation is multi-dimensional, but here I am largely thinking of money making. Few remember that as many as four out of the ten Companions of the Prophet who were congratulated as they were promised a place in Jannah died billionaires, in today's terms. There is ample evidence that they worked hard for that kind of wealth, especially as some of them, like Abdur-Rahman ibn Auf, had migrated to Medina empty handed. To the possible query, why earn so much? The answer that Islamic history provides with reference to men like Abdur-Rahman ibn Auf and Uthman ibn Affan, the celebrated third Caliph, lies in the last of the above sequence: giving.

Unfortunately, the self-confidence that makes a conscientious Muslim a big money maker in a life by definition transient and desired to be lived in preparation for the eternal life in the Hereafter was soon lost under the influence of Christian asceticism and, possibly, Greek and Hindu Philosophies. A shadow was cast upon "earning." This raised alarm bells among the wise and the farsighted, inviting a spate of works titled *The Book of Earning*, beginning with *Kitab al Kasb* by Imam Muhammad bin al-Hasan al-Shaybani(d.189 H/834 C.E.). These books, numbering a dozen over the next hundred years, argued in the light of texts from the Qur'an and Sunnah that it was all right for a Muslim to earn, save, and invest. The first generation of Muslims had a vision of living that precluded the need for such arguments. Going further into this probe will, however, take us far from the limited scope of a foreword, to a book making a plea for Muslims to take their finances seriously. Suffice it to say that something bigger than your pleasure and the felicity of your progeny is at stake.

Convince Muslims that they need not be very keen to earn and you have knocked the bottom out of the whole edifice; pulling down this one pillar threatens the whole structure with collapse. Sounds strange in twenty-first century America, where everybody is going crazy after earning. Well, have a second look at the recipe: earn, save, invest, spend, and give. Many Americans spend before they earn. Do not do that, the author says, as our beloved Prophet was averse to indebtedness, so much so that his supplications to God included seeking protection from being in debt. Reported supplications associate heavy indebtedness with bondage (*ghalabat al-dayn*).

Some venture to give without having saved and invested. Not sustainable, warns our money manager. You have to plan for giving in an efficient way. The idea of efficient giving should be pursued further; indeed organized philanthropy deserves a chapter in all textbooks on Islamic economics. *Zakah, waqf,* and charitable giving in general provide an important complement to market economy in Islam. The focus in the book is on how to calculate zakah-liability. The next step is how to organize zakah expenditure at community level so that its place in a fully functioning Islamic economy may be defined, where the state too plays a significant role besides the market and the voluntary sector, based on giving.

The "five pillars" of prosperity indicated by the author need not be envisioned as a straight path. Instead, they form a ring as the one on your finger. Earning-saving-investing enables you to spend and also creates an obligation to give; the urge to give prods good people to earn more, save, and invest. In between comes spending, which gives you comfort while boosting growth. It is a virtuous circle. Be serious about the entire circuit, if you want the current to flow and electrify your life.

The young Islamic community in North America will greatly benefit from the wealth-building strategies suggested by the author. It is a timely contribution. The community is passing through trying times when money would serve it well. I know of no other person better equipped than Dr. Yaqub Mirza to perform the *fard al-kifayah* of telling Muslims how to manage their finances.

Mohammad Nejatullah Siddiqi
Professor Emeritus, Faculty of Business Administration
Aligarh Muslim University

Preface

While helping my father in our family business (I was 12 years old), I studied books of the Hadith (sayings of the Prophet Muhammad, peace be upon him), which my father had in his library. Studying these books was a great learning experience in every respect. We discussed work ethics, the virtues of hard work, being persistent to achieve results, helping the needy, and supporting social services that are in keeping with one's faith.

While discussing the concept of debt, my father used to remind me that God will forgive through His mercy everything except debt and wrongs done to others. These, he said, could be forgiven only by the aggrieved party, and on the Day of Judgment if they do not forgive you, then God will take your good deeds to recompense them.

This left a great impression on me. Growing up, I became very conscious of debt and wanted to avoid borrowing money and hurting someone's feelings. I vividly recall times when I was making a purchase and I had only part of the money; the shopkeepers (they knew me, as we were living in a small town) would say take the merchandise and pay the rest later. I would decline, telling them to hold the merchandise until I had the money to pay first; the thought being that if I took the item—while owing money and I died (on my way home)—my family wouldn't know I owed this money. "This will be a debt which I will have to deal with in the Hereafter."

This became a guiding principle in my life that pushed me to find ways for my family to pay for a car, a house, Hajj, my children's education, etc., without incurring debt (and paying interest). This led me to the study and practice (and ultimately putting this guide together) of the five key elements of money:

EARN—SAVE—INVEST—SPEND—GIVE

This approach requires a lot of discipline, patience, and fortitude, and if you put in the effort to incorporate these in your life, you will soon achieve wealth and peace of mind, without financial worry.

Hopefully, by following this approach, you will soon have enough money to enjoy life and help others. Enjoy.

M. Yaqub Mirza
Washington, D.C.

Acknowledgments

While the idea for *Five Pillars of Prosperity* was inspired by what my father taught me, the book quickly took on a life of its own. This deeply collaborative effort has evolved over the past few years to what I hope provides a spiritually grounded approach to building wealth in one's life.

First and foremost, I would like to thank my family and colleagues (including those at Sterling Management Group) for their encouragement and support in this effort amidst multiple priorities, as well as the many thought leaders who graciously agreed to share their views, insights, and lessons learned about wealth and its preservation.

Second, I would like to thank Salma El Kadi Abugideiri for suggesting that I put my ideas down on paper, Allison Lake for her assistance in putting together the initial draft, and Yousuf Anis for his continued support of this and other ongoing projects.

I would also like to extend my sincere appreciation to Chris Grant of the Lazarus Group for designing the narrative framework and developing the process that guided the manuscript to completion. Without his help and devotion this book would not have been possible. I am grateful for his assistance and friendship.

I thank the many friends who took the time to review and comment on the book, as well as Dr. Hisham Altalib, Dr. Ahmad Totonji, Dr. Abdul Hamid Abu Sulayman, and Dr. Taha J. Al-Alwani for their encouragement and support.

And finally, I'd like to thank Dr. Jamal Barzinji for his review of the book, as well as invaluable advice, contribution, and friendship.

Introduction

In today's climate of economic distress and uncertainty, people the world over have seen their assets and savings greatly diminished. Yet, as the Qur'an points out, with crisis comes opportunity: "Surely, with every difficulty there is relief" (Q 94:5–6). The recession has caused many to adopt a "back to basics" approach to finances. As individuals, families, and businesses struggle to regain the prosperity they once enjoyed, it has become more important than ever for them to master and control their finances. Many are now reconsidering the use of credit cards and borrowing even to cover essential life expenses. People are seeking ways of managing money that ensure consistent financial security while avoiding risky ventures and heavy borrowing of any kind.

This book presents the Islamic approach to finance, which is based on commonsense principles. As Muslim scholar Irfan Ul Haq notes, Islam promotes the work ethic and private economic enterprise and urges the creation of wealth. Islam favors accumulation of wealth through saving and investment, and recycling of wealth through reinvestment on a continuous basis. It simultaneously discourages conspicuous consumption and suggests modest living. Islam argues that society should operate responsibly, work hard, and produce a caring and prosperous community. Taking care of its poor and needy and behaving ethically are at the heart of Islamic values.[1] The Holy Qur'an encourages believers to engage in beneficial trade and to invest. In it, God encourages Muslims "not to eat up your [wealth] among yourselves in vanities: but let there be trade amongst you by mutual goodwill" (Q 4:29).

Financing that follows Islamic principles is relatively risk-averse. It focuses on building wealth for the long term in a way that does not put money in the pockets of creditors or in the hands of companies that are unethically directed. Islamic financial principles also prohibit purchasing or investing in any industry or company associated with vices such as alcohol, tobacco, gambling, and pornography, and they prohibit charging interest on loans.

Islam, perhaps more than any other major religion of the world, sees finance as integral with faith. For centuries, Muslims all over the world have directed business enterprises; financed ambitious and innovative projects; traded across deserts, oceans, and continents; and provided for their families in ways consistent with Islamic principles.

Islamic financial principles are based on Shari'ah law. With the help of jurists (Muslim legal scholars) Muslims employ a sophisticated understanding of economics as well as unique ways of making transactions to further their financial goals.

A financial system following Islamic principles is known as Shari'ah compliant. To be compliant, a transaction must not contradict the scriptures, although a transaction does not have to be mentioned in the scriptures to be acceptable. Any law that supports what is good and moral is considered Islamic. As long as it follows the values of justice, preservation of equity, and fairness, then the transaction is valid. The transaction must also use proper currency and be without ambiguity.

Living a Shari'ah-compliant financial life is a challenge for Muslims living today in Western cultures, where Christianity and Judaism predominate and financial culture and practices do not entirely support the Shari'ah-compliant financial principles of Islam. For one thing, Christianity includes a theme of otherworldliness and puritanism: "Do not store up for yourselves on earth . . . but store up for yourselves treasures in heaven. . . . (Matthew 6:19–20). However, there are also many in Christianity who question this and support a view closer to that of Islam.

Gary Moore (who runs a financial seminary) writes, in *Faithful Finances 101*, that religions such as Islam, Judaism, and Christianity "abandoned the field of economic morality to the secular world."[2]

> Economic *negativity* has impoverished Christianity and our world in many ways. Fear closes the hand around what one has. While that may be beneficial to those who are spending too much, it is

devastating to those who have excess and need to invest or give that excess, rather than hoard it. It is even more devastating to those who need those investments.[3]

However, Moore says, "we can't separate our economic and political lives from our morality and spirituality."[4] He encourages "integrating our faith with all that we do," and noticing "how the world of commerce and the world of faith shape human affections, depositions, and practices."

Moore quotes Sir John Templeton as referring to an "attitude of gratitude" as a way to adopt a more holistic ethic in finances.[5] Following a similar approach, Moore writes that "in order to be faithful to our finances, we must resolve consciously to use *all* of God's wealth—100 percent of the time, talent, and treasure with which we have been entrusted—for the glory of God as well as for the benefit of others and ourselves."[6]

The Qur'an says, similarly: "Seek with the [wealth] which God has bestowed on thee, the Home of the Hereafter, nor forget your portion in this World: but do thou good, as God has been good to thee, and seek not [occasions for] mischief in the land: For God loves not those who do mischief" (Q 28:77).

"And ordain for us that which is good, in this life and in the hereafter, for we have turned unto thee" (Q 7:156); and "Eat of the good things that We have provided for you and be grateful to God, if it is Him you worship" (Q 2:172).

Muslims in North America and Europe *can* live according to Islamic financial principles, especially as existing financial institutions begin to offer appropriate programs and new institutions are created to specifically meet Muslim needs. They can earn their living, deposit their savings, finance their cars and homes, insure their assets, charge their purchases, and make investment choices for their future and the future of their children in accordance with Islamic teachings.[7]

Shari'ah law is clear on certain key financial principles, including avoiding debt; neither earning nor paying interest; and the ethical use of wealth for supporting first oneself and one's family, then the larger community. We will look at these one by one.

Refrain from Borrowing and Incurring Debt

Islam prefers that a person not be in a dependent position, so Muslims are strongly discouraged from incurring debt. Certainly giving in charity or spending for social welfare is better than being a recipient. A debt-free Muslim who saves wisely can then have enough money for a car, a college education, marriage (one's own or one's child's), *hajj* (pilgrimage), and *umrah* (travel to Mecca outside the pilgrimage season).

Lynnette Khalfani-Cox in her book *Zero Debt* states: "Debt is the longest-lasting economic curse, the most heinous financial plague, and the least recognized form of modern slavery afflicting Americans (and others around the world) this millennium."[8]

Borrowing cannot be taken lightly. Borrowing by individuals and businesses may be necessary and beneficial in some situations, although arbitrary overextension is not a healthy practice.[9] If a person spends only a part of what he earns and practices moderation in his living habits and controls his spending, it is unlikely that he will be compelled to borrow.[10] If you must borrow, borrow moderately, and strive to repay the debt as soon as possible and continue to maintain more assets than liabilities (i.e., positive net worth). Go too much into debt and you will find yourself discredited.

The Prophet Muhammad disliked it when people were in debt because debt worries the mind at night and is humiliating by day. It is recorded in the *hadith*, the record of the sayings of Muhammad, that he always asked God's protection from "the burden of debt and from the anger of men."[11] The Prophet also said he sought refuge in Allah (God) "from unbelief and debt," and that he equated debt with unbelief.[12] In his prayers, he frequently said, "O Allah, I seek refuge in Thee from sin and debt." He was asked, "Why do you so often seek the protection of Allah from debt?" He replied, "One who is in debt tells lies and breaks promises."[13]

The Prophet also stated that financial indebtedness may lead to *kufr* (rejection of God's teachings) or immoral behavior.[14] He would not say the funeral prayer for a person who had died in a state of indebtedness and did not leave behind enough property to repay his loans. He did this to discourage others from such an end. He led their funeral prayers after either he or the community collectively paid off the debt. He said, "Everything will be forgiven to the *shaheed* (martyr in the cause of Allah) except debt."[15]

The Muslim who is informed of these hadith understands that he should not resort to borrowing except in the case of dire need, and if he does borrow, he must remain mindful of the obligation of repayment.

The Prophet strongly urged those able to repay the debt they had incurred to do so quickly and without delay. A hadith states, "If a man borrows from people with the intention of repaying them, Allah will help him to repay, while if he borrows without intending to repay them, Allah will bring him to ruin."[16]

At the same time, the Qur'an teaches us to have mercy on the debtor.[17] "If the debtor is in difficulty, grant him time till it is easy for him to repay, if you remit it by way of charity that is best for you if you only knew" (Q 2:280).

Avoid Interest

Another element of the Islamic principles regarding finances is its prohibition regarding interest. Both paying and receiving interest are prohibited in Islam.

The word *riba*, translated as "interest" or "usury" by different authors,[18] literally means increase, addition, expansion, or growth. In Shari'ah, riba technically refers to the "premium" that the borrower must pay to the lender, along with the principal amount, for postponing, deferring, or waiting for a payment of the loan.[19] Riba includes both simple and compound interest. It refers to any money made on money, in contrast to money made by working or trade or by investing through equity partnership on a profit-loss-sharing basis.

Riba in a loan is considered unjust, especially when the lender and borrower enter into an agreement on unequal terms, or when the lender is guaranteed a profit regardless of whether the borrower gains or loses money on the transaction.[20] With an interest-bearing loan the borrower repays the lender more than he has borrowed and previously received from him. Thus riba is like unearned income in biblical terms; the lender "reaps where he did not sow."

The Qur'an teaches about riba: "Devour not usury [riba], doubled and re-doubled" (Q 3:130). "O you who believe, Fear Allah, and give up what remains of your demand for usury, if you are indeed believers. If you do it not, take notice of war from Allah and his Messenger. But if you turn back, you shall have your capital sums; Deal not unjustly and you shall not be dealt with unjustly" (Q 2:278–279). "He [Allah] has explained to you in details what is forbidden to you except under compulsion of necessity" (Q 8:119).

This prohibition against interest also rules out interest-bearing investments, including conventional money market or money market mutual funds, certificates of deposit, corporate bonds, and US Treasury bonds or T-bills. Some scholars have permitted sovereign bonds (*sukuk*), especially in Muslim countries.

The Jewish law with respect to interest is more qualified, permitting interest on a loan to a stranger but not on a loan to another Jew. It says: "On loans to a foreigner you may charge interest, but on loans to another Israelite you may not charge interest" (Deuteronomy 23:20). And: "If you lend money to my people, to the poor among you, you shall not deal with them as a creditor; you shall not exact interest from them" (Exodus 22:25).

The New Testament, on the other hand, reflects the commercial practices of the Roman Empire because Rome ruled in that part of the world during the lifetime of Jesus. Thus the New Testament assumes the legitimacy of banking, credit, and interest: "Then you ought to have invested my money with the bankers, and on my return I would have received what was my own with interest" (Matthew 25:27).

Meet the Needs of Family

While Islam supports the accumulation of wealth, it is clear regarding the proper use of this wealth: first to take care of the needs of oneself and one's family. The family bond among people bound together by blood ties and/or marital relationship entails mutual expectations of rights and obligations that are prescribed by religion and enforced by law. Accordingly, family members share certain mutual commitments. These pertain to identity, provision, inheritance, counsel, affection for the young, security for the aged, and maximization of effort to ensure continuity of the family.

My wife and I consider education to be the most important investment in the future growth and accomplishment of our children. When it came to our children's educational pursuits, we did not want to force our children down a particular career path (say to be a doctor or a physicist). Instead, we simply encouraged them to discover their God-given talents and gave them the support and freedom to pursue and excel at them. We let them know that we expected them to excel in whatever they chose. While we controlled family expenditures, we sought to provide them ample resources with regard to education (such as educational games and toys, computers, courses in speed-reading and -writing, speech therapy, etc.). The children were encouraged to look into any resource that would help them develop their skills, and when they found it, our typical response was: "go for it." We are grateful for God's blessing and are seeing positive results from these investments.

In general, parents worry about their children having access to credit cards, bank accounts, and cash. We had the same concern with our children, and while we provided them access to these financial resources, we made a great effort to teach them how to use these resources properly and to be financially responsible. We felt that the only way they could learn about money was to have access to it. Our goal was to empower them to use these resources without fear—to be comfortable having access to money that they can spend but decide not to! It is the best way to teach them money management; how else will they learn not to spend if they do not have money?

In order to serve our family we as parents sought to do things that ensured the continuity of our family by establishing a Family Limited Partnership (FLP). This FLP serves not only as a vehicle for family investments, but also as a kind of cooperative, helping each member as needs arise. The partners (family members) meet occasionally to discuss the business of the partnership. Within this partnership, family members are bound together not only by the bond of blood ties but also through "financial ties." This will hopefully preserve and sustain the members of the family. By executing the responsibilities that come from managing this FLP, the partners are learning about investment possibilities, how to "work out" their differences, and how to keep the family together. The spouses of our children are also welcome to participate in these discussions and enjoy these resources.

We fully realize the challenges our children may face as the family grows and matures, but we are quite confident that our children will live up to this challenge. They have seen how we work out our differences while keeping our faith and family strong and united.

One of the actions the family took was to have an open discussion about our core family values. Each family member was present and contributed to the discussion and finally we created the following (family) mission statement:

> Our family aspires to live from the highest levels of sincerity, humility and integrity, guided by a deep spiritual relationship with Allah (swt) through (the joy) of Islam. We express this commitment through: the caring & nurturing of each other's growth (in body, mind and soul); showing each other our love for one another through our generosity, mercy and forgiveness; fostering a spirit of collaboration and community activism; and continuously striving to better ourselves individually and as a family.

We found having a mission statement helped us to foster and sustain unity and focus, and I highly recommend to all families to create a mission statement of their own.

We as a family are thankful to God for all He has bestowed on us, and promise to live as good citizens in pursuit of peace, freedom, and liberty, while sharing with those who are in need.

Give Support to Community

After the immediate family receives benefit from these resources, and when any extended family (for example, aunts and uncles, in-laws, cousins) who are in need have been helped, our assistance should then extend to the larger community.

For Muslims living in North America or Europe today, the larger community includes people of other faiths, particularly the other two Abrahamic faiths, Judaism and Christianity.

These three religions are naturally suited to coexist and even to mutually reinforce each other. As one author explains:

> Being originally one religion, the three Abrahamic faiths worship the same God, although the three religions may differ in how they conceptualize that one God. God made this very point in the Qur'an when He said that the Muslims and the People of the Book [*ahl al-kitab*; i.e., Jews and Christians] have the same deity: "our God and your God is One; and it is to Him we bow [in Islam]."[21]

Few non-Muslims are aware that the Prophet Muhammad, the messenger of Islam, preached that Jesus and Moses were the pre-Islamic bearers of God's revelation to mankind. Islam recognizes both the Torah and the New Testament, and texts from these scriptures are cited in the Qur'an. As Christians believe the New Testament was the completion of the "Old Testament" of Judaism, so Muslims believe the Qur'an is the final completion of these books, and Muhammad is the last Prophet and Messenger of God.[22]

Judaism, Christianity, and Islam are all monotheistic religions, namely, they believe that there is only one God.[23] Jews and Muslims greatly stress the oneness and unity of God. The affirmation of the oneness of God by Christians is sometimes misunderstood, because many Christians believe that the one God is triune (the Holy Trinity). However, this is not a denial of monotheism but an affirmation of the complexity of their understanding of the Divine Being.

All three religions believe that this God, the origin and source of all that exists, is just and also merciful. He has provided basic rules for our guidance so that we may be good and righteous, and by His grace we are given the strength to be righteous.

Judaism, Christianity, and Islam also share common rituals and practices (such as regular prayer and charity). All three value pilgrimage and share many common holy places; promise that behavior will receive its proper rewards and punishments in the future, on earth and in an afterlife; and balance and integrate strands of mysticism, legalism, and pious devotion.

Love of God and love of one's neighbors are the two great commandments in Judaism, Christianity, and Islam. The New Testament says: "Love the Lord your God with all your heart and with all your soul and with all your mind and with all your strength. Love your neighbor as yourself" (Mark 12:30-31).

The essence of Islam is to serve Allah and do good to your fellow-creatures. This expands on the theme of "Love God and love your neighbor." It includes duties to animals as our fellow creatures and emphasizes service in addition to sentiment.

As the Qur'an says: "Serve Allah, and join not any partners with Him; and do good—to parents, relatives, orphans, those in need, neighbors who are near, neighbors who are strangers, the companion by your side, the wayfarer (you meet), and what your right hands possess: For Allah loveth not the proud and boastful ones" (Q 4:36).

Many hadith enjoin good treatment of neighbors in general, regardless of whether they are relatives or not—and whether they are of the same religion or not. For example, the Prophet said:[24] "Jibreel [Gabriel] kept urging me to treat neighbours kindly, until I thought that he would make neighbours heirs."[25]

The *Sahâbah* (Companions) heard this teaching of the Prophet, and they hastened to put it into practice in their daily lives with their own neighbors, both Muslims and non-Muslims. 'Abdullah ibn 'Amr, the great *Sahâbi* (Companion), remembered this hadith when he slaughtered one of his sheep, and he asked his servant, "Did you give any to our Jewish neighbor? Did you give any to our Jewish neighbor? For I heard the Messenger of Allah say . . ."—and he quoted this hadith:[26]

"He does not believe in me who goes to bed full when his neighbor beside him is hungry and he knows about that."[27]

The Qur'an repeatedly calls for universal cooperation among all races, peoples, and tribes. Muslims must deal kindly and justly with all those who have different beliefs from theirs, as long as they are not at war against Muslims on account of their faith nor have driven them out of their homes (Q 60:7-9).

These comments about the commonalities among the three Abrahamic religions are about similarities of faith and ethics. Similarly, the interfaith movement, which may include not only Jews, Christians, and Muslims but also Sikhs, Hindus, Buddhists, and others, has generally been focused on sharing scripture. However, the core commonality we all have is not in our understanding of what God is or is not, but in the fact that we all live together on earth.[28] My friend and religious scholar Joseph Montville has beautifully expressed this interfaith perspective as follows: "The community may also include those who profess no religion, but still reflect God's guidance in their lives—individuals whose number would greatly expand the community. In the end, it is God only who judges who is worthy of salvation regardless of professed faith or none."[29]

The larger community is built around our shared love of God and love of the planet. Service to nature is the bond that connects people of all faiths. The environmental movement offers Muslims, Christians, Jews, and other faith congregants the opportunity to connect in a spirit of service to our shared earth.

There are several charitable organizations (like FAITH: Foundation for Appropriate Immediate Temporary Help, located in Herndon, Virginia) striving to foster understanding and acceptance among adherents of the Abrahamic and other faiths. One such organization is the Centre for Abrahamic Religions. This center is the result of a collaborative effort among Durham University and Cambridge University in the United Kingdom and the University of Virginia in the United States. The center, through its Scriptural Reasoning program, seeks to acknowledge and discover the commonalities and distinctiveness of the Tanakh, the Qur'an, and the Bible.

While I am not trained in nor do I profess to interpret the scripture, I do envision a world in which we the people find the ways and means to "commune." I accept the fact that others have no wish to convert to Islam but are willing to learn from one another and live in peace and harmony. It may not be easy, but I believe this is the only way we can all progress and coexist as human beings on this planet Earth—to live in a compassionate "global community." We must treat others like we ourselves wish to be treated.

Today's Need for the Five Pillars of Prosperity

The global community of today is both fortunate and challenged. We are experiencing a proliferation of opportunities available to more people than ever before in history. At the same time, we live in a world that is obsessed with money: acquiring it, possessing it, and spending it (and sometimes showing off too!). The purpose of money is to serve as a medium of exchange for goods and services. In today's world, however, it has come to represent power and prestige. For the typical person money serves as a means to define his/her identity (i.e., "I am a millionaire . . . ")

Having (or not having) money should not define who we are as a person. In reality, if you make the mistake of allowing money to define you—it will enslave you. Instead of working for a living, you'll end up living to work. In most societies around the globe, there is a growing desire to consume and acquire things. The world's marketers (and the businesses they represent) are busy developing more effective and clever means of getting you to desire things that separate you from your money and possibly your future happiness.

Historically, many institutions—through the world's media (advertising; marketing), banking and finance systems—have encouraged, cajoled, enticed, seduced, and conditioned us to be blind consumers. They generate profit by incentivizing citizens to spend their future earnings through incurring debt. Sadly, we've become desensitized to physical money, and we are being encouraged to use credit cards, debit cards, and other electronic payment systems instead of physical money. This has caused many people to become impulsive buyers, paying for things today against money earned at some future date. This is a rat trap—one that can be quite destructive. Many people have become victims to the ill practice of "buying things you do not need with money you do not have," resulting in unnecessary borrowing and living it up with someone else's money.

In 2009, the US economy was in a deep recession, with the debt of the US federal government exceeding 15 trillion dollars just three years later. Rather than setting the example for sound financial planning, the US Congress has taken the opposite tack, choosing to put off making the hard choices involving austerity and fiscal discipline in favor of short-term gains. This approach has created a host of problems for Americans. American workers and business owners are facing levels of uncertainty about the future that haven't been seen since the Great Depression. No one knows if the US government will ultimately default on its debt, or how stable their investments will be in the future, or whether there will be a sudden collapse of the US stock market.

All of this uncertainty underscores the need for citizens to take responsibility for insuring their own financial well-being, and it's my hope that the information provided in this book will assist the reader with this imperative.

There is a way out.

The way out is to understand and then build your financial life upon the five pillars of prosperity: to become masters of earning, saving, investing, spending, and giving.

This guide can be used as a starting point, and the time to start the process is today. In the following chapters we will discuss each of these elements in detail:

> **Pillar 1: Earning.** This is the key element that supports the other four; we'll discuss the three levels of earning or money creation.

> **Pillar 2: Saving.** This is the key element that ensures that we become good stewards over the money that flows into our lives. Through the practice of "delayed gratification," it conditions us to be in control of our overall financial health.

Pillar 3: Investing. Mastering this element will give us the ability to actively use our money without consuming it. It teaches us how to manage our surplus earnings and put this money to work for our future (cash flow) needs.

Pillar 4: Spending. Mastering this element helps us master cash flow and budget and control spending, and insures that we avoid addictive and impulsive spending due to outside influences (marketing manipulation, status, peer pressure, etc.).

Pillar 5: Giving. Perhaps the most important element to prosperity; this element teaches and encourages us to make meaningful contributions to individuals and our society and gives us an opportunity to exercise the best part of ourselves by supporting others for the greater good.

This five-step financial program can be summarized as follows:

According to Islamic financial principles, a person's first financial duty is to take care of the needs of self and family—to **earn** the money, to **save** it by keeping daily expenditures less than income, and to **invest** the money so it will increase. In addition to daily expenditures, one can plan in order to **spend** intelligently on big-ticket expenditures of a constructive nature, such as education and hajj. Finally, after the daily and big-ticket needs of family are met, one can **give** in order to help the larger community, as formalized in the Islamic practices of zakah and sadaqa, as well as other forms of giving while living.

In this book, you will find practical tools for managing money and building wealth. The approach in this book is faith-based, but one does not need to be Muslim to utilize this book and benefit from it.

How to Use this Book

I recommend that you read through this book chapter by chapter. Try not to skip chapters even if you feel you are already strong or knowledgeable in a particular section. After each chapter, in a journal or a notebook, write down three actions you will take as a result of what you read. These actions may be academic actions (to seek out further information for study, for example), or they may be concrete actions (opening an investment account, writing a will, investing in a mutual fund, writing a budget, etc.).

For those of you who are young (teenagers, young adults), I recommend that you study the guide with a friend or a group of friends or a family member (spouse, parent, or sibling). The fastest way to learn is to teach and then practice: take the chapters and divide them among your group. While everyone will read every chapter, the person that is assigned a chapter has the responsibility to present the "key points" or takeaways that they identify from the chapter. This will help make the concepts quickly "sink in," and, in time, become an integral part of your thinking and habits around personal finance.

How the Prophet Muhammad Implemented the Concept of Pluralism

The Prophet established the first pluralistic, multi-faith state. The state of Yathrib, which was founded by the Messenger, was formed of various groups of people, who are mentioned in the text of the Saheefah, a kind of "Constitution," which was drawn up by the Prophet. This was similar in many ways to the modern political concept of the state, which is defined by the groups living in the state and the land where they live.

The Prophet did not restrict his community to only one group that followed one particular religion. He included in it the Muslims who had migrated from Mecca (the *muhajirun*), the Muslim inhabitants of Medina (the *ansar*), and the Jews who were with them. He said concerning all of these people in the Saheefah: "They are one nation, distinct from other people." This concept is now known as pluralism or described as a multi-cultural community.

Allah willed that this new Islamic state should be recorded for the first time in history in a constitutional document that was approved of by all parties.

Lay congregations can come together and work together. This work will consist of radically altering our way of thinking about development, profit, gain, and loss. We need to connect with those of other faiths to raise our children as part of a larger community of "people of faith." We make these connections through establishing community gardens, engaging in cleanup efforts, renovating or replacing old buildings, and salvaging useful materials.

One such example is the Masjid At-Taqwa in Brooklyn, New York. When Imam Siraj Wahhaj and his colleagues purchased the building at 1266 Bedford Avenue in Brooklyn back in the early 1980s, it was an abandoned clothing store. Their first job was to expel the drug users and dealers. Thanks to joint efforts between the police and Muslims organized by Imam Wahhaj, the area was successfully reclaimed from drugs and crime. Today, the "mosque of God-consciousness" serves as a symbol of the neighborhood's flourishing "Muslim economy," which includes a deli, a convenience store, and a Halal restaurant.[32]

"Those who have faith and do righteous deeds—they are the best of creatures" (Q 98:2).

1 | Pillar One: Earning

"Far and away the best prize that life has to offer is the chance to work hard at work worth doing." –Theodore Roosevelt

In the twenty-first century, earning—the ability to generate income—is more complex and fluid than at any other time in history. While the principles surrounding investing and business ownership have largely remained constant, employment and what it means to be employed are undergoing significant changes. Within these changes lie earning opportunities for those who have the eyes to see them and the courage to act on them.

Earning, the first pillar of prosperity, makes prosperity possible; it is the foundation upon which the other four pillars are built. Earning is thus fundamental to our livelihood.

Means of Livelihood and Sustenance on Earth

The Qur'an points to the matter of livelihood as inseparable from being alive as a human being.[1] It states: "The earth will be your dwelling place and your means of livelihood for a time" (Q 2:36; see also 7:24). This verse addresses Adam and Eve, but it is applicable to all humankind for all times. The Qur'an further says that our means of livelihood is given by God: "It is We who have placed you [humankind] with authority [or ability] on earth, and provided you therein with means of fulfillment of your life [ma'ayash]: small are the thanks you give" (Q 7:10). Similarly, "And [We] have provided you therein means of subsistence for you [humankind] and for those for whose sustenance you are not responsible" (Q 15:20).

We acquire our livelihood through work. One of the Qur'anic principles is that "man can have nothing but what he strives for" (Q 53:39). This has a spiritual meaning and it also has a worldly meaning: earnings come through work, and when a person works he or she will see the fruit of that effort, which will be fully rewarded in Heaven (Q 53:39–41).

The Qur'an uses several terms when referring to work: *'amal* (work), *kasb* (earning), *sakhkhara* (to employ or utilize), *ajr* (wages or reward), and *ibtigha'a fadl Allah* (seeking God's bounty for creating wealth). The Qur'an sees work—both manual and intellectual, as well as the combination of the two, which is the usual case—as the primary means of acquiring income, property, and wealth. It insists that people should work: "And say: Work (*i'malu*), soon will God observe your work . . ." (Q 9:105). This command to work is universal, not conditioned by time, and applicable to everyone.

As is evident from this verse and also verse 34:13 ("Work you!. . ."), work has moral value. All of one's actions will be judged (rewarded or punished) on the Day of Judgment, including one's work. Therefore, work is necessary not only to meet personal and family needs and wants, but also to demonstrate one's moral worth.

The Prophet clearly emphasizes the importance of working and earning a livelihood in the following words: "To strive to earn a livelihood through the right means is an obligation after the obligation of prayer," and "Bread earned by one's own labor [or effort] is the best of all earnings."[2]

We are meant to work and earn our livelihood during the day. The Qur'an explicitly points this out: "It is out of His mercy [or grace] that He has made for you the night and the day, so that you may rest [at night] and that you may seek of His bounty [during the day]; and [He has given you all this] in order that you may be grateful" (Q 28:73; also 17:12). Also, "made the day as a means of subsistence [for you]" (Q 78:11), and the following: "And among His signs is the sleep that you take by night and work by day" (Q 30:23).

The Qur'an implies that all seven days are open for work except Friday, the day of communal gathering (*yawm al-jumu'ah*), during the time when the Jummah prayers (around noon) are performed. Once the prayers are completed, we should return to work. "And when the prayer is ended, then disperse in the land and seek of Allah's bounty, and remember Allah much, that ye may be successful" (Q 62:10). The Qur'an does not ask Muslims to abstain from work during the month of Ramadan (the ninth month in the Islamic lunar calendar), during which fasting from dawn to sunset is an obligation upon all healthy adult Muslims (Q 2:185). It even permits the combining of work with religious duties like hajj (pilgrimage) (Q 2:198).

The Social Function of Wealth

Along with valuing work, Islam places a high value on the cultivation of wealth that results from work.[3] Acquiring wealth is necessary for performing the religious duties of *zakah* (obligatory giving) and hajj. So also, voluntary social contributions (*sadaqah*), which are critical for the support and growth of society, cannot be made without wealth. However, the value Islam places on accumulating wealth should not be construed to mean that those without wealth are less worthy than those who have it.

Some people argue that acquiring wealth is not good, that one should just focus on the worship of God. On the contrary, as Irfan Ul Haq points out, the Qur'an associates the earning and creation of wealth with God's bounty, grace, and good (*al-khayr*).[4] The Prophet clearly views acquiring wealth as praiseworthy because it makes it possible for the earner to support society through activities such as feeding the hungry, taking care of the needs of widows, and supporting orphans and the poor.

First and foremost, Islam requires the individual to earn and accumulate sufficient wealth to satisfy his or her own needs and the needs of his or her family. This follows from the Qur'anic command to work and the Qur'anic injunctions to support one's wife and children. Numerous traditions of the Prophet affirm this principle. For instance: "Every man is a guardian of his family and is responsible for it."[5]

The responsibility to provide healthy maintenance of oneself and one's dependents is not only a worldly obligation but also a religious duty toward God and society. Islam regards life as sacred and its preservation as a moral and legal obligation, and this includes support of one's dependents at a reasonable level. No effort should be spared in the fulfillment of this primary function.

After the needs of self and family are met, an individual should consider how any additional wealth can be used to help others. A minimum level of goods production within a community is necessary to ensure everyone's needs are fulfilled. Islam also encourages trade to acquire necessary goods that cannot be produced locally, or at least not cost effectively.

Islam regards the purpose of economic enterprise to be the fulfillment of society's material and service needs—easing homelessness and hardship, and establishing justice and prosperity for all. Helping to accomplish this is considered *fard al-kifayah* (socially obligatory) for Muslims. At the same time, according to a Prophetic tradition, it is open to each human being to determine how much to contribute to society, be it little or more, and in what form, be it wealth, stature, or personal capabilities. Whatever the amount and form, this contribution is counted as a rewardable charity both in this world and in the hereafter.[6]

Although the New Testament may not be as explicit as the Qur'an and the Prophet Muhammad regarding the importance of acquiring wealth for benefiting society, some modern Christian writers do address this point. One such author, Wayne Grudem, says:

> "The ability to earn a profit is thus the ability to multiply our resources—while helping other people. It is a wonderful ability that God gave us and it is not evil or morally neutral but fundamentally good. Through it we can reflect God's attributes of love for others, wisdom, sovereignty, planning for the future, and so forth."[7]

Grudem also points out: "We could use our resources to advance our own pride, or we could become greedy and accumulate wealth for its own sake, or we could take wrongful security in riches (Matthew 6:19; Luke 12:13-21; James 5:3). We could use our possessions foolishly and wastefully, abounding in luxury and self-indulgence while we neglect the needs of others (James 5:5; John 3:17)." However, he says, "These things are called 'materialism,' and they are wrong."[8]

At the same time, Grudem says, the social teaching of the Church insists that businesses must also safeguard the dignity of the individual, and that even in moments of economic difficulty, business decisions should not be guided exclusively by considerations of profit. "We can imitate God's attributes each time we buy and sell, if we practice honesty, faithfulness to our commitments, fairness, and freedom of choice."[9]

The Prophet is clear that those capable of earning should not allow themselves to become a burden on society but should remain productive, earning members of society who contribute to the community's well-being and economy. That is why the Prophet prohibits healthy adult men from begging and from receiving zakah under normal circumstances. He affirms the dignity of labor—any kind of labor—and the indignity of depending on the dole of others: "It is better for anyone of you to take a rope and cut the wood [from the forest] and carry it over his back and sell it [as a means of earning his living] rather than to ask a person for something and that person may or may not give him."[10]

Yet, as Irfan Ul Haq points out, this should not be taken to imply that only working-age people and their dependents should be fed, clothed, and sheltered.[11] Sometimes, in spite of their hard work, people may not earn enough to meet their own needs. Or, due to infirmity, age, or another handicap, they may not be capable of earning and may not have a family member who can take care of their needs. For such people who are financially strapped, God has decreed receiving charity in the form of zakah as their means of livelihood.

Earning Money

In today's society, money is essential for living. Livelihoods are earned and wealth is accumulated and shared in the form of money. Because of money's importance, many people regard it as a form of protection from harm and hardship, which encourages a "survival-based" attitude around money. But basing one's survival on something—in this case, money—that is outside oneself causes apprehension or fear. This is the reason for the anxiety around money that is rampant in society today.

In fact, money is simply a medium of exchange. What fundamentally keeps us alive is our faith, vitality, and strength of spirit—not money.

Money is a medium of exchange in return for value given. Our ability to generate money is directly linked to our ability to generate value in the lives of others. This value may be given to a person, a company, a project, or an enterprise.

In general, the more the world values what you generate, the more money will be given to you. However, not all value is equal. There are essentially three factors that determine your ability to generate money through providing value:

- The uniqueness (or possibly exclusivity) of what you are offering

- The "footprint" of what you offer, that is, the number of people who benefit from it

- The impact your offering has on someone else

The degree of value you offer with regard to each of these three factors determines the amount of money you receive in exchange.

What kinds of activities are involved in earning money? Basically, there are three types: you make money for yourself, other people make money for you, and your investments make money for you. I will discuss these one by one.

You make money for yourself. The majority of the world's population earns money by making it for themselves. People working in every job classification—whether they be doctors, engineers, pilots, gardeners, grocery clerks, or factory workers—trade their time for money. The challenge with this method of earning is that a person's time is finite—and thus so is the person's income. Hence, if you become unable to trade your time for money, you've lost your source of income.

Other people make money for you. For small-business owners and other individuals involved in entrepreneurial pursuits, revenue and ultimately profit are generated by the activities of the business and the efforts of its employees. This makes better use of the business owner's time, since the time of several people is focused on earning money for the business and, ultimately, for the owner. It is also more stable, since if one person cannot work, others are present to take up the slack. Small-business owners and other individuals involved in entrepreneurial pursuits fall in this category.

Your investments make money for you. Earning a profit on investments is the optimal earning strategy, although only a small percentage of the world's population effectively uses it. Using money to make money requires knowledge and skill—and money. Sadly, most people, whether due to lack of knowledge, living paycheck to paycheck, or for other reasons, are unable to earn money through investments. That said, many people can eventually earn money this way if they follow the five principles outlined in this book. Here again, the key ingredient, besides money, is *time*, since the length of time the money is invested factors significantly in the success or failure of most investments.

In the rest of this chapter, I discuss employment and entrepreneurship, which are often, though not always, aligned with the first two methods of earning money: making money for yourself and other people making money for you. The third, earning through investing, is discussed in chapter 3.

Employment

The great majority of us start out our professional journey employed. But I would advise the following: While working as an employee, start seeing things with the eyes of an owner. Whether your employer is a big or small company, take the opportunity to experience and grow as much as possible. Learn to become aware of what impact your work has on the organization's success, and you will start to develop an appreciation for things beyond your job.

For example: If you are paid $65,000 income, depending on your benefits (health, 401K, training reimbursement, vacation, etc.) your actual compensation can be up to 36 percent more on average (when you factor in payroll taxes, health insurance, office overhead, and other benefits). This means your employer is actually paying closer to $90,000 in total compensation to you. Since the business cannot run on a deficit, your contribution must be generating at least what they are paying you. Ideally, your contribution converts to some multiple of what you are being paid.

My advice to younger readers aspiring to have a successful career, who may be contemplating eschewing more traditional professions for the latest and greatest, such as high technology and other highly visible and apparently lucrative endeavors, is this: be diligent in your research of any career track you are considering. You may want to read Richard N. Bolles' *What Color Is Your Parachute?* book series. It provides a practical and systematic approach to discovering career and job choices that would be most appropriate for you. Books like *What Color is Your Parachute?* are extremely helpful to anyone wishing to change jobs or career tracks as well.

My personal motto has been "If someone else can do my job, then I am not doing my job." We must persist and excel at what we do and, hopefully, do it better than others.

Entrepreneurship

With the development of information technology and the growth of the internet as a marketplace, it is becoming easier for more people to become entrepreneurs. As this entrepreneurial trend grows, it is essential that people of faith take leadership roles as entrepreneurs. The world needs business owners who can ensure the call of God as they help build and lead society through faith-based businesses.[12]

The combination of faith and entrepreneurship has been modeled in Islam from its very beginning. The Prophet Muhammad himself was an influential and successful businessman and a trader. He was known for always charging fair prices and never hoarding any goods. Because of this, the people of Mecca dubbed him *Al-Sadiq* and *Al-Amin* (the Truthful and the Trustworthy).

Abdur-Rahman ibn Auf, an early believer and Companion of the Prophet, was born in Mecca and became a Muslim when he was thirty years old. He then migrated from Mecca to Medina, where he started his business and soon became the wealthiest merchant in Medina.

Uthman bin Affan, the third Caliph, learned to read and write at an early age, and as a young man became a successful merchant. His generosity had no limits. On various occasions, he spent a great portion of his wealth for the welfare of the Muslims, for charity, and for equipping the Muslim armies. That is why he came to be known as *ghani*, meaning "generous."

Imam Abu Hanifah (d. 767 c.e./148 a.h.), founder of the Hanafi school of law, was born into a family of tradesmen. He earned his living through trade and used his earnings to meet the needs of his students. He gave much to charity. Every Friday he would distribute twenty gold coins to the poor for the benefit of his parents' souls.

The Bible also describes several entrepreneurs, including Peter, Paul, and Job.[13] Peter was a commercial fisherman in partnership with his brother Andrew (Matthew 4:18). Paul was the sole proprietor of a tent-making business (Acts 18:3). Job was an industrious farmer who owned seven thousand sheep, three thousand camels, five hundred oxen, and five hundred donkeys, leading to his launching businesses in wool clothing, freight hauling, and dairy.

One reason the world needs people of faith in business is because their faith guides their ethics. The business practices of Muslim entrepreneurs must be above reproach, because they are obliged to follow the business principles outlined in the Qur'an:

Do not engage in bribery or dishonesty (Q 2:188)
Deal justly in business or trade (Q 38:24)
Document and witness agreements (Q 2:282)
Do not engage in fraud or deception or mismeasurement (Q 83:1-3)
Give everyone his due share (Q 4:33)
Do not engage in hoarding or exploitation (Q 10:58)
Be kind (Q 5:13)

The Prophet Muhammad emphasize ethics in business. He urged Muslims to be truthful in all business dealings, to honor their promises, to negotiate honestly, and not try to lower the value of goods by berating another's merchandise nor inflate the value of their own goods through exaggerated claims. He told Muslim entrepreneurs not to avoid payments they owe, and when others owe them to not make it difficult for debtors to repay them.

Having served on the boards of several publically traded companies, I can attest that the temptation to deviate from ethical practices is always present. For example, reporting one cent more profit per share on a company's profit-and-loss statement could mean a stock price increase of twenty cents. And if one owns 100,000 shares or options, that translates to a $20,000 (assuming a P/E [price/earnings] of 20) gain. But we stick to our creed, not the greed.

Passion, Creativity, and the Entrepreneur

The social and economic environment in America provides excellent opportunities for people of faith to be successful in business and shape the future of the world we live in. The success of the democratic capitalist system stems from freedom of ideas, creativity, and invention. Those with a natural ability to see what is around them differently and then move beyond conventional thinking and ways of doing things have historically provided the driving force for invention, change, and success in America.

If you are an individual who is willing to take a risk to start a business, works tirelessly, has abundant energy, foresees change, develops new products to take advantage of that change, uses innovations (in technology, processes, or marketing) to take those products in new directions, and is committed to growing fast without being overwhelmed with the possibility of failure, then you have the makings of an entrepreneur. In my experience, the most successful entrepreneurs are those who strive to succeed from a foundation of passion and unwavering belief in what they are trying to create. It's this passion and belief, along with prayer, that allows them to persevere through the inevitable challenges that occur along the way.

Another important element in the success of an entrepreneur is creativity. One of the greatest gifts God has bestowed upon human beings is our ability to imagine. It's astounding how creative and inventive we can be when it comes to pursuing a dream or an idea.

The Qur'an views the creation of ideas and the pursuit of knowledge as activities of the highest value. It advises: "Say 'O my Lord! Advance me in knowledge'" (Q 20:114). Conversely, the Qur'an tells us to turn away from the ignorant (Q 7:199). It says that humankind's existence and superiority over all other creatures is based on the human faculty for understanding and knowledge as well as the freedom and ability to use it (Q 2:30–33). Knowledge enables humans to lead an enlightened life and to fulfill the purpose of creation by fulfilling the will of God. The Qur'an says: "And say: My Lord! Increase me in knowledge" (Q 20:114). "Verily in this is a sign for those who give thought" (Q 16:69). "Verily in that are signs for those who reflect" (Q 30:21). "That man can have nothing but what he strives for" (Q 53:39).

Muslims, along with all people of faith, must invent and innovate. They must find new ways of doing things better, easier, cheaper, smarter, and faster. They should come up with more efficient products and services to win global markets. It is always safe to assume not that the old way is wrong but that there may be a better way.

The Prophet Muhammad said, "God has decreed that for everything there is a better way."

Social Entrepreneurship

An aspect of entrepreneurship that may be a good fit for people of faith is social entrepreneurship. In this form of entrepreneurship, which is a growing movement worldwide, a for-profit venture exists to generate income for a social purpose. For example, an independent for-profit venture might donate its profits to charity. Or a company or other large enterprise might hire less-privileged or unemployed workers to provide services or create a product.

Social entrepreneurs often take on society's most pressing problems. They may serve as change agents for the masses, exploiting opportunities that others miss, improve systems, and develop creative, scalable solutions that improve society. Recent examples of social entrepreneurs are Muhammad Yunus, founder of Grameen Bank (Bangladesh), a microfinance organization and community development bank that provides small loans to the poor; and Istvan Aba-Horvath, whose mission is to aid Gypsy children in Hungary in getting an education while earning money.

Then there are social entrepreneurs such as Muhammad Bah Abba, who has resurrected a form of pottery used in ancient Egypt that allows his people to keep their food fresh in the harsh climate of Nigeria; and Rafael Alvarez, who founded Genesys Works, an organization that helps American youth extend their outlook beyond high school graduation by training them in highly skilled jobs.

Questions for Aspiring Entrepreneurs

Over the years, aspiring entrepreneurs have asked me, in one form or another, the question: "What should I pursue?" I always answer them with a series of questions, which I share here:

1. In what areas are you most gifted and talented?

2. Where do your passions lie?

3. Where are you starting from? (What experiences, resources, connections, etc., do you have to work with?)

4. What product or service do you want to offer and to whom?

5. Is there a demand for this product or service, and if so, is it already being met? If not, why not?

6. Have you done a needs assessment or a feasibility study?

7. How exactly will you make money from this venture? (From whom? How much? When?)

8. How serious are you? (What steps have you already taken? What research have you already done?)

9. What's your motivation for doing this? (Perhaps the most important question.)

Armed with answers to these questions, the person can look at the myriad of ideas out there and quickly identify one or more that resonates with his or her skills, passion, and beliefs.

Another method of determining preferences may be to conduct a SWOT analysis. This involves listing and analyzing your Strengths, your Weaknesses, the Opportunities available to you, and the Threats (lack of experience, lack of capital, competition, etc.) that you face.

Entrepreneurship is not limited to those with lots of previous experience in business or as an employee. A younger person with passion, commitment, and willingness to learn can succeed just as well, as the stories of many of the most successful startup companies show. Paul, the apostle, encouraged Timothy, a young person: "Let no one look down on your youthfulness, but rather in speech, conduct, love, faith and purity, show yourself an example to those who believe" (I Timothy 4:12).

Eight Qualities for Success

Regardless of whether you choose a traditional means of employment or decide to strike out on your own as an entrepreneur, I've found that the following are key attributes that many of the most successful people possess.

Gratitude—This is perhaps the most basic—and important—attribute, upon which all others are built. In my humblest opinion, people who possess this attribute tend to be some of the most extraordinary people that will ever walk the earth, and it's an attribute that can readily be obtained and cultivated in every human being. All of the Abrahamic faiths speak to the importance of gratitude, of being grateful. People possessing gratitude enjoy not having to succumb to greed or envy but instead largely operate from love, appreciation, and generosity.

An additional benefit to possessing this attribute is that you can avoid the traps that come from being too prideful. It's one thing to take pride in one's work and appreciate one's accomplishments, and it's quite another to have so much pride that you're seen as boastful or vain. Too much pride can be like a cancer, one that can hurt and consume a person without creating any meaningful benefit. I believe gratitude is the precursor to the attainment of true "wealth" in one's life. Always have an attitude of gratitude.

Strong Work Ethic—Having a strong work ethic means being willing to do what must be done 100 percent of the time. It can sometimes mean that you are faced with having to endure doing difficult work for a long duration of time. But it also means approaching one's work with both dignity and intelligence. Your work ethic is a reflection of your "soul," the very essence of your being; give the world your best efforts, put in an honest day's work, even when no one appears to notice.

The Qur'an is constantly encouraging the Prophet to strive hard in the cause of Allah: "And those who strive in Our [cause], We will certainly guide them to our Paths: For verily God is with those who do right" (Q 29:69).

Focus—When I think about management, leadership, and an organization at large, another key attribute I'm constantly seeking (for both myself and others) is an ability to focus. "Focus," in my view, really suggests *mindfulness*: being fully present in the moment with the task or objective in hand. Not allowing for outside distractions that can have detrimental effects on the quality of your work and the perceived (and real) contributions that your work has in the organization you work for (or own). Some of you may be asking yourselves, "focusing on what?" To focus merely for focus' sake isn't very useful: you should strive to avoid merely "being busy" versus achieving meaningful work (and thus value) for both yourself and the company you represent. Focusing on the most meaningful work will require being willing to be strategic in your approach towards your work as well as expending effort to set priorities (on your time and effort). Being seen as someone who is focused implies that you are careful, conscientious—and motivated. From a career-building perspective, having both focus and ambition together is a powerful combination and can lead to great opportunities.

Persistence—Even with the strongest commitment, intent, and motivation, despite one's best-laid plans, there are times when success can seem elusive and practically unattainable. In such times, one has to have the ability to persist—the willingness to sustain one's effort through continual trial and experiment, until the desired outcome is accomplished The most successful often find themselves in situations requiring not only patience but persistence, and the more persistent you can be, the more likely it is that good fortune and other opportunities will unfold for you.

And He provides for him from [sources] he never could imagine. And if anyone puts his trust in Allah, sufficient is [Allah] for him. For Allah will surely accomplish His purpose" (Q 65:3).

Successful indeed are the believers who are humble in their prayers (Q 23:1–2).

But remember the LORD your God, for it is he who gives you the ability to produce wealth, and so confirms his covenant, which he swore to your forefathers, as it is today (Deuteronomy 8:18).

O ye messengers! Enjoy (all) things good and pure, and work righteousness; for I am well acquainted with (all) that ye do (Q 23:51).

Passion (aka "Ambition")—Having passion for what you do for a living can do more good for your career than almost any other thing. Finding ways to deeply enjoy what you do, being inspired to learn and explore the depths of your chosen profession, can lead to new discoveries, new skills and abilities, and new interests and career directions, expanding opportunities and choices. If you're lucky, you sometimes can discover your passion first, with skill and expertise coming afterwards. But I find that one discovers what one is passionate about after first becoming really good at something, so don't despair if you haven't "found" your passion yet. Loving what you do often comes after being very good at what it is you do.

Integrity—I think having integrity—something that I hope is instilled in every child growing up—is absolutely paramount to one's success at being a valued member of mankind. Being true to your word—being impeccable with your word—trumps the most ironclad contract. Having integrity implies that one is a person who takes responsibility for one's commitments, obligations, and promises seriously. In fact, being a person of integrity is the ultimate contract, and conducting business (as an entrepreneur) or contributing to an organization from a place of integrity will give you access to near unlimited opportunity.

High Standards—A person who has high standards (for both oneself and others) is a person who seeks and is striving for excellence. A person who chooses to have high standards tends to avoid mediocrity and instead works to be, do, and have the best in everything. As a young adult, this means striving to gain access to the best educational resources one can afford, seeking the best mentors one can find, and doing the best that one can do in any give moment. Just as success breeds success, seeking the best in everything tends to attract the best in everything.

The Prophet said, "God loves when one of you is doing something that he [or she] does it in the most excellent manner."

Generosity of spirit—giving credit where credit is due; humbleness; appreciating others. Fairness and kindness—dealing with people in a fair way—go a long way without taking undue advantage of others in a moment of weakness. Kindness includes avoiding talking down to people or taking a superior position to another person.

Serve others—When you experience success, don't forget how you obtained it. Even while you are climbing the ladder of success, be willing to serve others.

Income Management

As important as it is to earn money, it's equally important to manage what's earned. In particular, it's vital to establish strategies for handling both increases and decreases to your income when they happen.

An increase may be due to a raise, promotion, or salary increase if you are employed, or due to the growth of your business if you are an entrepreneur. An increase can also happen through tax refunds, gifts, or receiving an inheritance. A decrease in income may be due to a job layoff or because of periodic smaller earnings in your own business. Other causes include disability, a natural disaster, or relocating in order to care for a family member who is ill. Without a strategy in place, a person may have difficulty riding through these ups and downs in one's income stream, which are normal and to be expected.

In some ways, an increase in income is more challenging to manage than a decrease. Without a plan in place, people are more likely to view the increase as a windfall. They feel this money is "extra money," so they expand their lifestyle—buying a new car or a "bigger" house, going on a vacation, and the like—which effectively consumes the increase. Living without a plan or a budget and not understanding where your money is really going, you will automatically increase your daily, weekly, and monthly spending, leaving you with the same amount of net earnings as prior to the increase. If you have assumed new debt obligations, you may have even less.

My recommendation if you experience an increase in earnings is to resist changing your lifestyle for at least six months to a year (and preferably, not change it at all). Give yourself a chance to live with this new income and see how it factors into your saving and investment goals before you make changes. If you don't take the time to adjust to the increase, you'll consume all of it and won't know where it went.

Another good rule of thumb is to spend 10 percent of this new money (you'll consume this amount with some kind of purchase), apply 30 percent of this new money to ongoing obligations (e.g., cost-of-living expenses), and bank the remaining 60 percent in savings or investments.

With a little planning and discipline, you can apply these increases intelligently. Here are a few ideas: pay off debt obligations, invest the money in something long-term, pay down or eliminate a home mortgage, or gift all or part of the increase to parents or other family members as a way to share in the pleasure of additional income.

2 | Pillar Two: Saving

Islamic economic doctrine emphasizes hard work, productivity, and the generation of surplus.[1] The surplus makes possible saving, whether for future contingencies, posterity, or other purposes—such as investing, making major purchases, or giving to help the needy and supporting projects of public good. Therefore, while the first pillar of prosperity is to generate sufficient income to meet the current consumption needs of the individual and his or her family, the second pillar is to generate savings.

Some people think spirituality and saving do not go together. But there is nothing unspiritual about having money set aside for investments and for future needs. This does not in any way show a lack of trust in God's provisions. Prophet Muhammad used to urge his Companions to be prudent by not spending all that they had.[2] The Qur'an recounts how, in times of plenty, Prophet Yusuf (Joseph) organized great reserves to meet the needs of famine (Q 12:47–49). Christian author Dwight Nichols points out in *God's Plans for Your Finances* that, according to the scriptures (Proverbs 6:6–8 and 21:20), a person who stores in times of plenty and prepares for winter is wise.[3]

The cornerstone of achieving financial freedom is the recognition that you are responsible for your own financial well-being, and the desire to save is the first step to financial freedom. The Qur'an also wants you to be cognizant of your own financial activities and their effects on yourself, your family, and others: "O you who believe! You have charge over your own souls" (Q 5:105). Unfortunately, too few people in America today are following this commonsense wisdom. Here are a few sobering statistics generated by Scottrade's 2011 American Retirement Survey:[4]

- Almost half (47 percent) of Baby Boomers (Americans born between 1945 and 1966) have $100,000 or less saved, and more than a third (37 percent) are concerned that they will have to work in their retirement years.

- Almost a quarter (23 percent) think they'll still be working at age 75 or older.

- A majority of Baby Boomers (58 percent) say that, if given a second chance, they would have started saving at a younger age.

- The majority (55 percent) of Gen Yers (Americans born between 1983 and 1992) have not started to save for retirement.

No one ever went broke saving money. Having more in savings means that money is available for college, vacations, retirement, and other long-term goals. In addition, the income from these savings may provide you additional cash flow that you may use at times of need or emergency.

Is a penny saved a penny earned, as Benjamin Franklin said? Not quite, because a penny saved is really equal to one and a half pennies earned; that is, it is the amount you would have *after* paying taxes on 1.5 pennies. How is this so? Federal, state, and sales taxes combined are approximately 33 percent. Therefore, $1.50 earned – .50 tax (33% of $1.50) = $1.00 net. So when you spend $1.00, pause and think, because you are really spending $1.50 earned. Conversely, if you cut expenses and save $1.00, you are really earning $1.50.

The key to being able to save is to engage in a profitable economic activity while maintaining a moderate level of consumption—in other words, to spend less than you earn. So this chapter focuses on saving by spending carefully on a daily basis. This involves moderation and balance.

The Qur'an commands that we be moderate in our living habits and thrifty in our financial affairs: "And do not squander [your wealth] wantonly; truly, those who squander are the brothers of the Evil Ones" (Q 17:26–27). "O Children of Adam, wear your beautiful apparel at every time and place of prayer; eat and drink; but waste not by excess, for Allah loves not the wasters" (Q 7:31). "And follow not the bidding of those who are extravagant" (Q 26:151). Islam encourages simple, modest living, not necessarily bare minimum subsistence.

The Qur'an condemns high consumption levels, opulence, wastefulness, and overindulgence in pleasures. The New Testament says, similarly: "And He said to them, 'Beware and be on your guard against every form of greed; for not even when one has an abundance does life consist of his possessions. For life is more than food, and the body more than clothing. For where your treasure is, there will your heart be also'" (Luke 12:15, 23, 34).

In recent years, the American public has seen a demonstration of the costs of unethical practices in business driven by greed. We watched executives lie, stock values plummet, companies (like Enron, MCI WorldCom, and Adelphia) implode, and jobs and investments disappear. When lies are woven into the fabric of financial life, that fabric will inevitably fray. It does not need to be this way. Sir John Templeton, investor and mutual fund pioneer, never used his wealth for a huge house, multiple residences, yachts, or private planes.[5] He was also thoughtful in his investment policy, avoiding the "sin stocks" belonging to alcohol, tobacco, and gambling companies (all items also prohibited in Islam).

Both the Qur'an and the Prophet Muhammad emphasize a balanced and moderate approach to solving problems, both spiritual and secular. "Believers are those who, when they spend, are not extravagant and not miserly but hold a just balance between those extremes" (Q 25:67). Balance (tawazun) is associated with justice, equity, and the practical dealings of life. A balanced approach in economic and financial matters discourages excess. Islam approves of lawful earnings, as well as lawful ways to save, spend, and enjoy life.

Living Debt Free

One of the keys to saving is to be free of debt. To stop being a slave to debt, you must stop the vicious, dead-end, no-win cycle of excessive spending. The average US household spends $1.22 for every $1.00 it earns. That's a recipe for a lifetime in debt.

Debt is strongly discouraged in Islam. Dr. Omar Clark Fisher says, "Muslims are urged in the Holy Qur'an and Sunnah to minimize borrowing and to repay financial obligations as soon as possible."[6] The Prophet is reported to have said: "O God, I seek refuge in Thee from disbelief and debt." When a man asked him, "Do you equate debt with disbelief?" he replied, "Yes."[7]

In another instance, when the Prophet said, "O Allah, I seek refuge in Thee from sin and debt," he was asked, "Why do you so often seek protection of Allah from debt?"
He replied, "One who is in debt tells lies and breaks promises."[8]

A few thoughts on moving towards debt-free living

During the research for the book, I've run across many sources offering suggestions on moving towards a debt-free life. Most of these suggestions fall in one of two camps. In one, most take what I would consider a technical approach to debt elimination—establishing (and living by) a budget, negotiations with creditors (to reduce or eliminate debt), and concepts like "debt acceleration." The other camp takes a more creative approach: coupon clipping, timing of purchases to exploit sales, bulk purchase schemes, and other means of "stretching" the dollar.

Both camps can lead you down the same road—a road of debt-free living. And for those of you who may find these strategies too extreme, what follows is a blend from both camps that I believe could serve you well.

Step 1: Assess your current debt picture. This is a vital first step: reviewing and listing all current debt (including personal loans). Until you have a complete and accurate picture of your debt situation, it will be very difficult to work your way out of it, so start with knowing where you are. When listing this debt, be sure to include the interest rate (if any), the due date (e.g., the tenth of each month) and the amount due for each payment. Once you've done this, review the list and do the following:

- Flag any debt you're not paying on a regular basis.

- Flag any credit-card debt for which you're only paying the minimum payment each month.

- Flag any debt on which you're consistently paying late (and incurring late charges).

Step 2: Reorganize your cash flow. This step will be especially useful for those of you who find that (1) you're making only the minimum monthly payments; or (2) you have most of your expenses "front-loaded" with income received at the beginning of the month (when rent or mortgage is typically due). Part of the challenge for people who are trying to break free from debt is that often all of the major expenses are front-loaded at the beginning of each month (rent, mortgage, car), with credit card and other installment debt often due several times each month, leaving one with the sense of never having any money and always under pressure to pay something.

Here is a strategy I recommend: arrange your debt payments so that with each paycheck, you are left with as much net income (after expenses) as possible. Here's an illustration:

A Typical Scenario...

1st of Month

Income (paycheck)	$ 1,684	
Rent		850
Car		265
Utilities (gas, electric)		80
Car insurance		75
Student loan		85
Credit card 1 (minimum payment)		48
Credit card 2 (minimum payment)		28
Totals	**$1,684**	**$1,431**
Net Income	**$253**	

15th of Month

Income (paycheck)	$ 1,684	
Cable/TV/Internet		124
Cell phone		75
Transportation (fuel, metro)		250
Food		300
Totals	**$1,684**	**$749**
Net Income	**$935**	

A Typical Scenario with debt re-organized

1st of Month

Income (paycheck)	$ 1,684	
Rent		850
Car		265
Student loan		85
Credit card 1 (minimum payment)		48
Credit card 2 (minimum payment)		28
Totals	**$1,684**	**$1,276**
Net Income	**$408**	

15th of Month

Income (paycheck)	$ 1,684	
Cable/TV/Internet		124
Cell phone		75
Transportation (fuel, metro)		250
Food		300
Utilities (gas, electric)		80
Car insurance		75
Totals	**$1,684**	**$904**
Net Income	**$780**	

As you can see, making just a few adjustments to the payment due date on some of the debt items provides more remaining net cash from your income across the entire month. Most of your creditors can easily accommodate a request to change the payment due date—in some cases you can do this from your account online and otherwise, a simple phone call can be placed to make this arrangement.

Step 3: Start living on a "cash-and-carry" basis. As you go about gaining control over your debt and cash flow, it's critical that you begin to conduct your life from a cash mindset. Leave the credit cards and debit cards at home (better yet—cut them up) and start carrying and using cash. For those of you who want or need to take baby steps—start with the debit card. You'll find that if you get in the habit of actually using cash, you'll automatically begin to cut down on impulsive purchases, because cash makes you sensitive to money that you have—and don't have—on you. It sounds simple, and it is, but for a lot of people, regaining this sensitivity to money really goes a long way to helping them break free from living in perpetual debt.

Step 4: Start saving money. This is the next critical step, because after you've organized your debt payment schedule and have smoothed out your net income, you have to quickly establish the habit of saving your net income. It doesn't matter whether its $25, $50, $100, or more you save—the important thing is getting in the habit of consistently saving income. Eliminating debt without the savings habit just means you'll have more money to spend—and still have no savings. The key here is saving money.

So, as you begin to repay and eventually eliminate your debt, get in the habit of saving the money that would normally have gone to that retired debt. Any bonuses, pay raises, and the like—save it. Try to delay increasing your lifestyle to consume the pay raise and instead sock it away.

Step 5: Increase your net income. After you've gotten in the habit of consistently saving, managing your bills and cash flow, it's time to take things up a notch. Review your list of creditors, specifically credit card, really any debt that has an interest payment attached to it, and set aside some time to contact each one of these creditors to see if you can get your interest rate lowered. As a rule, I would suggest contacting these creditors at least once a year to inquire about and request a lower interest rate. In many cases (especially if you are consistently paying on your bills) they will accommodate you and lower the rate. In some cases, they may even offer to lower the overall amount you owe and/or offer to accept a lump-sum payment that is less than the actual outstanding amount. There is a range of possibilities, but the most basic step and goal should be to request and receive a lower interest rate, which effectively lowers your payments and overall indebtedness.

Step 6: Create a spending plan (aka: "budget"). The sixth and last core step towards debt-free living is to come up with a plan—a plan for the rest of your life. After reducing and/or eliminating your debt, then what? Well, to answer this question involves taking time to sit down and think about your life and the management of this life. And the beginning step towards management (and eventual mastery) is planning. At this stage, you've created enough momentum and real results that you can see, touch, and feel regarding your finances and now it's time to beginning planning. Creating a spending plan or a budget insures that as your income grows, your wealth and your life-style will grow steadily and at a measured pace, as you all the while avoid overconsumption and falling into a debt trap.

The problem of indebtedness is being tackled by many communities, including religious communities. Reverend DeForest Soaries Jr., senior pastor of the First Baptist Church of Lincoln Gardens in Somerset, New Jersey, has made a commitment to his congregation to help them clean up their financial lives through the church's revolutionary program "dfree." The foundation of the dfree program is the elimination of three things: debt, delinquencies, and "deficit living," or not living within one's means. These three objectives are reinforced through dfree's "Say Yes to No Debt" pledge[9]:

I pledge:

- To use God's strategy for managing money
- To keep my expenses below my income
- To pay my bills on time
- To invest in assets that grow in value
- To contribute to my church and its ministries [community]

Reverend Soaries says, "There are many definitions of freedom. Given the avalanche of bankruptcies, foreclosures, and high-interest credit card debt that many people are experiencing, there may be no greater need than to understand the value and joy of debt-free living. There may be no greater legacy we can leave our children. Our ships [fortunes] can come in if we make a commitment to debt-free living and teach our children how to manage money and invest in their futures."[10] Other religious communities, including temples and mosques, could adopt similar programs to help members be financially responsible.

Developing a Plan in Order to Save

Saving is a practice of delayed gratification, a way to postpone consumption until a future time when it will be more enjoyable or more needed. To achieve this involves directing your choices away from satisfying immediate desires and toward the accumulation of long-term, income-producing assets. This is the core of building your net worth and economic progress.

We do not have to (and we should not) spend everything we earn. Instead, it is essential to plan ahead. It is better to live below our means now and reap the rewards later.

Your net worth is your assets minus your liabilities. You can increase your net worth by earning more, cutting expenses, minimizing (or removing) debt, saving regularly, and achieving a reasonable rate of return on investments. To do this involves setting up a plan for savings, as described in this section. The steps of the plan are: set financial goals, develop and live by a budget, track day-to-day spending, and get a handle on monthly income and expenses.

Set Financial Goals

A personal wealth-creation strategy is based on specific goals. Most people who have built wealth didn't do so overnight. They became wealthy by setting goals and striving to reach them.

In preparing your goals,

- be realistic;
- establish time frames;
- devise a plan; and
- be flexible, since goals can change.

As an example, Joseph set two short-term goals: to save $5,000 a year for five years to have $25,000 for a down payment on a house, and to pay off his $3,000 credit card debt within two years. He also set two long-term goals: to save and invest enough to have $25,000 in fifteen years for his children's college education, and in twenty years to have $50,000 saved toward retirement.

In the space provided, you can list your own top short-term and long-term goals:

Short-term Goals:

1._____

2._____

3._____

Long-term Goals:

1._____

2._____

3._____

Now you can choose how you will meet those goals. This is where budgeting comes into play.

Develop a Budget and Live By It

When it comes to budgeting, people generally fall into one of the following groups. Where do you fit in? Knowing what kind of financial manager you are will help you determine what changes to make.

Planners control their financial affairs. They budget to save.

Strugglers have trouble keeping their heads above rough financial waters. They find it difficult to budget to save.

Deniers refuse to see that they're in financial trouble. So they don't see a need to budget to save.

Impulsives seek immediate gratification. They spend today and let tomorrow take care of itself. Budgeting to save is foreign to them.

Sarah, a single parent with one child, is a planner. Saving is important to her. She budgets in order to live on her modest income. She has a little PDA on which she tracks every dime she spends. When her son was born, she started investing every month in a mutual fund for his college education. She is proud to say that she controls her future. She has bought her own home and provided for her son, and she has never bounced a check.

Lina, by contrast, is an impulsive. Lina has a good job, makes good money, and lives a pretty comfortable life, but her finances tell a different story. She has no savings or investments, owns no property, and has no savings for retirement. Plus, she's got a lot of credit card debt, lives from paycheck to paycheck, and doesn't budget.

To maximize your wealth-creating ability, you want to be a planner, like Sarah. A budget allows you to

- Understand where your money goes;
- Ensure you don't spend more than you make; and
- Find uses for your money that will increase your wealth.

To develop a budget, you need to both track your daily spending and understand your monthly income and expenses.

Track Day-to-Day Spending

One day, Lina, the impulsive, realized that to create wealth she had to become more like Sarah and plan her financial future. To start, Lina analyzed her finances to see how much money she made and how she was spending it. She set a goal to save $175 a month to put toward creating wealth.

First, she tracked her daily expenses for a few days. She carried a little notebook with her for jotting down her daily spending, whether by cash or debit card, check or credit card. A page from her notebook is on the following page.

Table 2.1   Lina's Day-to-Day Spending

DATE	EXPENSE	CASH/DEBIT/CHECK	CHARGE
1/2	Breakfast, Get-N-Go	$3.56	
1/2	Coffee	.90	
1/2	Lunch		$6.75
1/2	Soft drink	1.25	
1/2	Gas for car		46.00
1/2	Drinks with friends	10.00	
1/2	Dinner	10.00	
1/2	Newspaper	.50	
1/3	Pancakes and eggs, Moonlight Diner	4.95	
1/3	Newspaper	.50	
1/3	Coffee	.90	
1/3	Lunch with coworkers		5.72
1/3	Dinner		15.00
1/3	Dress (clothing)		45.00
1/3	Soft drink	1.25	
1/3	Trip to the movies	15.00	
1/4	Breakfast	3.50	
1/4	Coffee	.90	
1/4	Lunch	5.75	
1/4	Cookies	1.25	
1/4	Newspaper	.50	
1/4	Birthday present	15.00	
1/4	Dinner		6.77
1/5	Breakfast	3.25	
1/5	Coffee	.90	
1/5	Soft drink	1.25	
1/5	Newspaper	.90	
1/5	Magazine	3.95	
1/6	Breakfast	3.25	
1/6	Coffee	.90	
1/6	Newspaper	.50	
1/6	Lunch	4.50	
1/6	Cookies	1.25	
1/6	Jacket		50.00
1/6	Video rental	3.95	

Table 2.2   Lina's Monthly Budget

	CURRENT INCOME	INCOME CHANGES	NEW BUDGET
Take-home pay	$2,235		$2,235
Overtime pay		$40	40
Pension, Social Security benefits			
Investment earnings not reinvested			
Earnings on savings accounts			
Alimony/child support			
Other income			
Total income	$2,235	$40	$2,275

	EXPENSE AMOUNT	AMOUNT REDUCED	NEW AMOUNT
Rent	$680		$680
Renter's insurance	20		20
Electricity	60		60
Gas	30		30
Water	25		25
Telephone	50		50
Cable TV/Internet service	55	−20	35
Insurance (life, disability)	0		0
Charitable donations	0		0
Credit card payment	25		25
Groceries	200		200
Clothing	130	−30	100
Day care/tuition	0		0
Car loan	300		300
Car insurance	75		75
Gas for car	145	−20	125
Meals out & entertainment	425	−100	325
Miscellaneous daily expenses	100	−50	50
Total expenses	$2,320	−220	$2,100
Monthly net (income – expenses)	$ −45		$175
Available to save or invest	**$ 0**		**$175**

Get a Handle on Monthly Income and Expenses

Lina used the information from tracking her day-to-day expenses to develop a monthly budget. She added up her monthly bills and added to them her monthly expenses, calculated from what she had tracked. She also calculated her monthly income.

When Lina reviewed her budget, she realized she was spending more than she earned. Lina knew if she were ever going to save $175 a month, she had to cut her expenses, earn more money, or both. So she started to work overtime at her company, which increased her take-home pay. She also bought fewer clothes, discontinued premium cable TV channels, carpooled to work to cut gas consumption, and reduced her spending on eating out, entertainment, and other miscellaneous daily expenses.

Tracking her expenses paid off. Lina successfully developed a budget that enabled her to save $175 each month (see page 32).

If Lina sticks to her budget, she will have $175 a month that she can

- put in a savings account;
- invest in a 401(k) retirement plan at work;
- invest in an individual retirement account (IRA or ROTH-IRA);
- invest in stocks or mutual funds; or
- use to pay off debt.

These are just some of the wealth-building choices that become available when you budget to save.

Specific Suggestions for Saving

An important aspect of saving money is establishing habits that promote saving. Gary Moore, in *Faithful Finances 101*, writes: "The first rule of making money is not to lose it. Take time with your family to sit down and make a list of how each family member can contribute to saving money each day."[11]

In her book *7 Money Mantras for a Richer Life*, Michelle Singletary recommends establishing several money-saving habits.[12] The first is to deposit money in a savings or "rainy-day" account. This fund should provide for the inevitable rainy day when an appliance breaks down, or for the monsoon of losing one's job, she said. You should make it a practice to put away money in the rainy-day fund when you receive bonuses, gifts, income tax refunds, salary increases, a windfall (such as an inheritance), or repayments of loans (return of funds you loaned).

She also suggests accumulating "good" assets, such as cash, investments, real property, and personal property (car, clothing, household goods, and furniture). At the same time, you should avoid accumulating bad assets (such as the junk accumulating in the garage or the self-storage unit, and other infrequently or never-used items).

Singletary also recommends that before making a purchase, you always ask yourself if it is a necessity or a want. Today, most of the major manufacturers, like Apple, are churning out interesting and highly addictive products every two years, stoking a perpetual desire and lust for the latest gadget. Ask yourself the following: "Is it really necessary for me to spend $200 every two years for a new cell phone?" Marketers regularly incorporate the latest advances in behavioral sciences to figure out how to compel and influence desire and need for their products, with many successfully convincing you their brand is an important part of one's "lifestyle."

Small expenses definitely add up, especially when we treat "wants" as "necessities." Starbucks's 2011 revenue was $11.7 billion (the equivalent of $37.36 for every American)—a clear indication of how much Americans are spending for "wants."[13] Singletary notes how high much of our daily spending can be, including expenses such as lunches, phone calls, restaurant meals, movies, bank charges, delayed payment charges, and so on.

Another point Singletary emphasizes is that cash is better than credit, and she encourages people to "avoid credit card craziness" unless you pay off your credit card bill each month. American business magnate Warren Buffett offers advice along the same lines: "Stay away from credit cards and bank loans and invest in yourself and remember: Money doesn't create man, but it is the man who created money."[14]

Singletary presents three other useful principles of sane money management: keep it simple; priorities lead to prosperity; and pay attention if you are immersed in a cycle of being tired because you are working too hard to pay your bills, at the expense of your time with family and friends.

Singletary's suggestions clearly support spending wisely, and spending wisely and in moderation is a key to being able to save. There are other behavioral changes that may not appear to directly affect our individual budgets. However, if everyone attempts to save money in these ways, our behavior can affect how much we are charged in the future for items such as utilities, household goods, and so on. Here are some ideas to save money, including several from Singletary's chapter "Penny Pinchers":

- Conserve water and electricity.

- Use only the hot water you absolutely need.

- Turn down the temperature of your water heater by 10 to 20 degrees.

- Use travel bargains and frequent flyer miles for perks and upgrades.

- Stock up at bulk stores on travel essentials and food prior to your trips.

- Turn off the lights at home, in the office, and in hotels (when not in use).

- Think globally: your behavior outside the home affects overall energy costs.

- Use the stairs instead of the elevator (good for health and saves energy).

- Turn up the thermostat in summer by 1 degree and down by 1 degree in winter, saving about 3 percent on your energy bill.

- Use environmentally safe laundry and dishwasher detergents.

- Unplug chargers and appliances when not in use (saves energy).

These ideas can be supplemented by many more. Take time to brainstorm other energy-saving and cost-saving ideas with your family and friends. Begin to practice them, and soon these new habits will become part of your daily routine. We must find new ways of doing things better, faster, and cheaper, resulting in more savings.

Warren Buffet gives the following advice:[15]

- Live your life as simply as you can.

- Don't be seduced by the brand label; instead wear things that are made well and are comfortable.

- Avoid wasteful spending.

- Manage your life and priorities so that you can live on less than you earn, saving 20% (or preferably 30% or more) on all that you make.

Turning Off the Lights:
Saving Two Cents Can Go a Long Way

Growing up, my siblings and I were trained to save money by cutting unnecessary expenses. In particular, my dad always stressed turning off lights. I remember my dad frequently coming into the living room, turning off any unused lights, and then turning to me and saying, "Younus, that's saving two cents right there." (My dad always made sure to turn off the lights in front of me and then explain to me why he was doing it.) Whenever I left the house and forgot to turn off the lights in my room, he would remember (even if it was hours later) to tell me that he had turned off my room's lights.

This constant reinforcement eventually had an impact on me, but I did not realize how much I had internalized the lesson of turning off the lights until I got married. My wife would sometimes come home to a dark house and perplexingly ask, "Younus, why are all the lights turned off except the one that you are using?" I would respond, "Ask my dad." I would find myself unconsciously going through the house turning off lights. Sometimes I would accidently turn off the light that my wife was using, leading her to exclaim: "Younus, I am using that light! Go find another light to turn off!"

But the biggest lesson I learned was that it wasn't good enough to save money for money's sake. I never saw my dad going through his bank account giddy with how much money he had. Rather the purpose of the lesson was so we could invest money in more important things, notably education and helping those in need. When it came to buying books or paying for college, my dad was always eager to help out. Whenever somebody needed assistance, my dad would take pride in being the one who was able to provide the support. Thus I learned an invaluable life lesson that I am now passing on to my kids: saving two cents now can eventually turn into helping others later.

– Younus Y. Mirza, Ph.D.

3 | Pillar Three: Investing

As Irfan Ul Haq points out in *Economic Doctrines of Islam*, accumulation of wealth for its own sake is highly undesirable. The Qur'an severely condemns the noninvestment, or hoarding, of wealth (Q 102:1–6; 104:1–9).[1] Instead, according to Islamic principles, once a reasonable amount of money has been saved, some portion of it should be invested.

Many people make the mistake of looking at investing as a means to becoming wealthy. In fact, true wealth cannot be "purchased"; it is, instead, a state of mind. Your wealth consists of not only material things but also less tangible things such as your health, your time, your relationships (with family, loved ones, and the community), your generosity, and your heart. The sole purpose of investing is to generate income.

Investing, besides increasing one's own wealth, has social value. Irfan Ul Haq comments on the benefits of both private and social investments. When savings are invested as private investments (through nonpublic markets), they create goods and jobs, generate income, improve the living standard, and bring monetary reward to the investor. For this reason, private investing is meritorious and rewardable in the eyes of God.

Similarly, when savings are invested as social investments (for the betterment of society), they benefit the recipients, meeting their immediate needs and raising their living standard while also adding to aggregate demand and creating jobs and income through the multiplier effect. Social investing is therefore rewarded several-fold while allowing the purification and "sweetening" (*tazkiyah*) of the investor's wealth.[2]

I learned the value of investing early on through personal experience. In the early 1970s, when I was a graduate student, I saved about $200 a month (65 percent of my income). When I became a postdoctoral fellow, this amount increased to about $500 a month. By 1980, I had accumulated around $53,000. These funds, which were invested at a 10 percent rate of return on average, grew to $120,000 by the time my wife and I built our house, and to $266,000 by the time our oldest child was ready to go to college. By continuing to add some portion of our savings to these funds over time, we had enough to cover college-related expenses for our three other children and part of the purchase price of our house and cars.

What makes investing over a long period of time like this so successful is the power of compounding, which is best illustrated by comparing the following three examples:

As a girl, Sana showed that she was smart and responsible, so her parents wanted to do something nice for her by securing her future financial needs, including retirement. When she turned fourteen, her parents decided to gift her $2,000 every year for the next five years. They invested the money in a stock mutual fund (investing in growth stocks that follow Islamic principles). The investment during those five years totaled $10,000.

At age nineteen, Maryam secured a good job. She wanted to save and invest her money, so she asked her uncle for advice. He suggested investing $2,000 each year in a mutual fund (investing in growth stocks). She downloaded the forms, carefully read the prospectus, and opened her account. At age twenty-seven, she decided to buy a house and stop contributing to this savings account, letting it grow without adding more to it. Her total investment during those eight years was $16,000.

Julie had student loans that she wanted to pay off. She was very conscious of saving, so at age twenty-seven she decided to invest $2,000 each year until she reached the age of sixty-five. Her total investment during those thirty-nine years was $78,000.

Table 3.1 compares the total accumulation of funds for each woman when she reaches age sixty-five, assuming a 10 percent annual rate of return. (This rate is not utopian, because historically, since 1926, US stocks have yielded an average rate of return of more than 10 percent.) By comparison, bonds (not recommended) have averaged 5 percent, with inflation averaging around 3 percent per year.

The lesson of this comparison is clear: Time plays two key roles in wealth-building activities. It is the determining factor in the effectiveness

Table 3.1 Comparison of Total Accumulation of Funds by Age 65

AGE	Sana Investing began at age 14 (10% Annual Return)		Maryam Investing began at age 19 (10% Annual Return)		Julie Investing began at age 27 (10% Annual Return)	
	INVEST.	TOTAL	INVEST.	TOTAL	INVEST.	TOTAL
14	$2,000	$2,200				
15	2,000	4,620				
16	2,000	7,282				
17	2,000	10,210				
18	2,000	13,431				
19	0	14,774	$2,000	$2,200		
20	0	16,252	2,000	4,620		
21	0	17,877	2,000	7,282		
22	0	19,665	2,000	10,210		
23	0	21,631	2,000	13,431		
24	0	23,794	2,000	16,974		
25	0	26,174	2,000	20,871		
26	0	28,791	2,000	25,158		
27	0	31,670	0	27,674	$2,000	$2,200
28	0	34,837	0	30,442	2,000	4,620
29	0	38,321	0	33,486	2,000	7,282
30	0	42,153	0	36,834	2,000	10,210
31	0	46,368	0	40,518	2,000	13,431
32	0	51,005	0	44,570	2,000	16,974
33	0	56,106	0	48,027	2,000	20,871
34	0	61,716	0	53,929	2,000	25,158
35	0	67,888	0	59,322	2,000	29,874
36	0	74,676	0	65,256	2,000	35,072
37	0	82,144	0	71,780	2,000	40,768
38	0	90,359	0	78,958	2,000	47,045
39	0	99,394	0	86,854	2,000	53,949
40	0	109,334	0	95,540	2,000	61,544
41	0	120,267	0	105,094	2,000	69,899
42	0	132,294	0	115,603	2,000	79,089
43	0	145,523	0	127,163	2,000	89,198
44	0	160,076	0	139,880	2,000	100,318

Table 3.1 Continued

	Sana			Maryam			Julie	
AGE	INVEST.	TOTAL		INVEST.	TOTAL		INVEST.	TOTAL
45	0	176,083		0	153,868		2,000	112,550
46	0	193,692		0	169,255		2,000	126,005
47	0	213,061		0	188,180		2,000	140,805
48	0	234,367		0	204,798		2,000	157,086
49	0	257,803		0	226,278		2,000	174,094
50	0	283,358		0	247,806		2,000	194,694
51	0	311,942		0	272,586		2,000	216,363
52	0	343,136		0	299,845		2,000	240,199
53	0	377,450		0	329,830		2,000	266,419
54	0	415,195		0	362,813		2,000	295,261
55	0	456,715		0	399,094		2,000	326,988
56	0	502,386		0	439,003		2,000	361,886
57	0	552,625		0	482,904		2,000	400,275
58	0	607,887		0	531,194		2,000	442,503
59	0	668,676		0	584,314		2,000	488,953
60	0	735,543		0	642,745		2,000	540,048
61	0	809,098		0	707,020		2,000	596,253
62	0	890,007		0	777,722		2,000	658,078
63	0	979,008		0	855,494		2,000	726,086
64	0	1,076,909		0	941,043		2,000	800,895
65	0	1,184,600		0	1,035,148		2,000	883,185
	Total invested = $10,000			Total invested = $16,000			Total invested = $78,000	
	Earnings beyond investment = $1,174,600			Earnings beyond investment = $1,019,148			Earnings beyond investment = $805,185	

of compounding income. And it is an ally with regard to your investment "time horizon," meaning that the more time you have to invest, the more likely it is that good years will offset bad years and your investment's return will come close to the long-term average that you expect.

The best way to build a sizeable estate is to start early. The next best way is to start at once. During a CNBC interview program with Liz

Claman, Warren Buffett said that he bought his first share of stock at age eleven, and he now regrets that he started too late.[3]

As a businessman, investor, and active member of the Muslim community, I am often approached by people seeking investment advice. While an in-depth discussion of investing is beyond the scope of this book, there are in fact quite a number of excellent books on the subject, which can be found in the bibliography section at the end of this book. What follows are several key pieces of advice I can offer about investing.[4]

Set Up an Investment Strategy

The first key piece of investing advice is to have a strategy. When it comes to investments, many people are simply confused. As often as not, their investments are nothing more than a haphazard collection that accumulated over time without careful planning, though each investment may have seemed good at the time of purchase. The results of a lack of planning can be risky, leaving people short of achieving important financial goals, such as having sufficient retirement income or money for their children's college education.

Selecting an investment strategy may seem like a difficult task. In fact, it is not so difficult. Focusing on your long-term financial goals (where you want to be in several years) is the starting point.

Step 1: Take your financial inventory. Pull out your financial records on stock investments, mutual funds, or other liquid assets. Add the value of your house or condominium. Search for hidden assets like retirement plans, IRAs (individual retirement accounts), life insurance policies, and so forth. Once you have located your assets, total them up. Then subtract any debts you have: mortgages on real estate, taxes you owe but have not yet paid, credit card balances, home equity loans. The resulting figure is your net worth.

Step 2: Create your emergency fund. Once you have completed your inventory, set aside an emergency fund, which should be about six months' expenses. You should not take even modest investment risks until you have accumulated enough funds to cover your basic emergency needs.

Step 3: Determine your risk tolerance. Next, determine the amount of investment risk you can afford to take. Generally, the longer it will be until you need your money, the greater the risk you can afford because you have the time to ride out temporary drops in the value of your investments.

On the other hand, if you will need your money soon—perhaps you are nearing retirement and will need the money to pay expenses—you should limit your investment risks. You do not want to take the chance of having to raise funds for living expenses at a time when the value of your portfolio is temporarily low.

Furthermore, if you are the sort of person who can't sleep at night because your portfolio is temporarily down even a little in value, then you should definitely limit the risk you take. Peace of mind is important.

Step 4: Create an investment portfolio. The next step is to construct a diversified portfolio that blends many types of investments in order to lessen the risk associated with limiting yourself to only a particular investment. A diversified portfolio might include several types of investments: stocks, profit-sharing funds, real estate, and precious metals. For the Muslim investor who desires to follow Shari'ah, many kinds of investments present a problem because the type of business type is unacceptable or the company pays interest. For this reason, stocks play an unusually important role for Muslim investors.

Of course, the Muslim investor must pay attention to the companies in which he or she holds stock to be sure they follow practices consistent with Islamic principles. This isn't always easy. Coca-Cola, for example, may appear to be simply a soft drink company, but it also has large holdings in the wine business, which is prohibited for investment by Muslims.

Consult an Investment Professional

Another key piece of advice for successful investing is to consult an investment professional. In fact, not working with a professional is often the primary reason people do not reap the full potential of their investments.

When people achieve a certain degree of success in a profession (say, in medicine or engineering or science), they sometimes assume they can be equally successful in making the choices that become available as a result of that success, including choices about investing. However, as Michael Mauboussin explains,[5] such overconfidence can lead to three illusions that can cause poor decisions: an unrealistically positive view of oneself, seeing one's own future as brighter than that of others, and behaving as if one can control, or at least influence, circumstances that one demonstrably has no influence over.

In fact, success in one's profession cannot guarantee success in other areas of one's life. Accessing investment opportunities and making investment decisions require special training and skills. Not everyone can be good at these tasks, just as not everyone can be a good doctor or engineer or scientist.

Not only that. Not all investment professionals are the same, just as not all doctors are the same. Some are excellent doctors, and others are not so excellent. For this reason, choose your investment professional as carefully as you would choose your doctor or lawyer or other professional consultant.

Above all, do not buy something just because an expert, such as the ones you see on CNBC, recommended buying it. Consider this: How will you know when that same expert will sell it?

Educate Yourself

Successful investing requires some effort to educate yourself. The best investors spend time learning about the markets they are investing in. While a good advisor is invaluable in guiding an investor's investment decisions, it is still up to the investor to understand what he or she is investing in—both the risks involved and the rewards. I can recommend several great books to help you get started. Burton Malkiel's *A Random Walk Down Wall Street* is a timeless classic, and Warren Buffett's *Berkshire Hathaway Letters to Shareholders: 1965–2012* reveals his views on business and investing. Peter Lynch's *Learn to Earn* is an excellent primer for young investors, while *The Intelligent Investor*, by Benjamin Graham, is an advanced book that may prove valuable once you have gained some experience with the markets.

Take a Consistent Approach

Another key to successful long-term investing is consistency. Most in-dividual investors tend to be market followers, investing when things seem to be going well and selling (or at least holding off on investing) when things don't look so good. However, following the market vio-lates the basic rule of investing: buy low and sell high. Unfortunately, it is hard to tell what "low" or "high" is in an investment context, so many people tend to time their buying and selling badly. In addition, many studies have shown that timing the markets accurately is extremely difficult. Even if you do a good job of market timing, you must be right most of the time to make it worth the trouble.

For the majority of investors, a consistent and disciplined approach is important. Select your strategy, stick to it, pick your investments accordingly, and make your investments consistently.

Seek Out Faith-Based Investments

In addition to developing an investment strategy, consulting a profes-sional, and being consistent with their investing strategy, investors who wish to follow the principles of Islam have special needs to be met. Following Islamic financial principles, Muslims tend to avoid speculation, in the sense of uninformed, undisciplined betting on the future. Many Muslims avoid futures contracts or investments that are not backed by a tangible asset or identifiable service. And Muslim investors want to their investments to be Shari'ah compliant.

Investment Vehicles for Muslim Investors

The remainder of the chapter discusses several key investment vehicles available today, including some that are especially appropriate for Muslim investors.

Real Estate: A Traditional Choice

Investing in real estate for the long term is a long-standing traditional way to accumulate wealth through increases in value of the asset and rental income. Investments in real estate usually start when a person buys a home to live in. People also invest in real estate in the form of vacation homes, waterfront properties, condominiums, and apartment buildings. They also buy investment units in publicly traded REITs (Real Estate Investment Trusts) or in private partnerships that own real estate.

When investing in real estate, a Muslim can try to ensure that the method of financing is Shari'ah compliant. For additional information on investing in real estate I recommend Virginia Morris's book, *A Muslim's Guide to Investing and Personal Finance.*[6]

Yet with real estate, as with any investment, there are risks. If the real estate market declines, one stands to lose. This is especially true if the real estate holdings are leveraged.

Buying an older property poses its own challenges because of the upkeep involved and the need to make sure the property conforms to current building codes. It is wise to do a comprehensive investigation into the operation costs, maintenance costs, and other costs (e.g., environmental costs, such as the cost of removing asbestos or lead from the property) before deciding to purchase such property.

Ramit Sethi, in his book *I Will Teach You to Be Rich*, realistically analyzes the pros and cons of buying a house.[7] Sethi quotes a comment made by Yale economist Robert Shiller: "From 1890 through 1990, the return on residential real estate was just about zero adjusted for inflation."[8] I have looked at the same charts from 1890 through 2011 and seen that the result is almost the same. Real estate prices peaked in 2006, but then turned right back down and are projected to decline almost to the level where they were when the boom started.[9]

Sethi comments: "Of course, there are certainly benefits to buying a house and, like I said, most Americans will purchase one in their lifetime. If you can afford it and you're sure you'll be staying in the same area for a long time, buying a house can be a great way to make a significant purchase, build equity, and create a stable place to raise a family."[10]

He suggests a conservative approach to buying a home—one should put a down payment of at least 20 percent, and get a 30-year fixed mortgage (I prefer 15-year mortgages) which should represent no more than 30 percent of the buyer's gross pay. The buyer should plan to live in this house at least five or ten years, preferably longer.

If you cannot do as Sethi suggests, then it is probably best to wait until you have saved enough money for the down payment. You can stretch a little but not too much.

The Role of Stocks in a Muslim's Portfolio

Common stocks play a major role in any long-term investment strategy. Owning stocks represents partial ownership of a business and a claim on the business's earnings and value over time. Although the value of stocks fluctuates with changing market conditions, successful businesses grow in value, and this growth generally results in higher stock prices.

As a successful company's earnings grow, they are either reinvested in the business to increase its value or paid out to shareholders as dividends. Stocks earn a return based on the company's success. Stocks are not interest-paying securities representing a loan, and therefore stock ownership is considered an acceptable instrument for Muslims.

Remembering that stock prices fluctuate, an investor should be careful to diversify, or blend, the investment portfolio across several companies and industries. Diversification diminishes the risk of a single company's stock price severely reducing the value of an entire portfolio.

One strategy that helps diminish fluctuations in the value of a stock portfolio is to invest in companies that have a record of paying consistent dividends. Because such companies are generally more mature, they tend not to have the growth potential of smaller, less mature companies. Companies that are rapidly growing and reinvesting every available dollar back into their growth can become very profitable. However, the less volatile stock price and steady payment of dividends of a mature, stable business often show up as a more stable portfolio value.

Mutual Funds: A Possible Solution

One way to get a desirable balance of growth, diversification, and income in a portfolio is with mutual funds. Mutual funds pool the assets of investors. They also provide the following for the individual investor: professional management services, buying and selling of stock in the portfolio, simplified record-keeping, lower transaction costs, and a well-researched investment portfolio.

Each fund has a different objective. A potential investor needs to read each fund's prospectus to be certain that its objective is in concert with his or her own. Some funds charge sales commissions ("loads") when stocks are bought or sold. The funds with no sales charges ("no-loads") represent the best value, since no money is going towards sales costs. Other funds say they have no loads but charge ongoing fees, called "12b-1 fees" (used to cover costs of marketing the fund), after the rule permitting them. These extra fees and charges add up. Read every fund's prospectus carefully and understand all the charges and expenses of the fund before you invest.

While no mutual fund can guarantee that it will achieve its objectives, by diversifying their investments mutual funds help reduce the risk of owning just a few securities. Before selecting a fund, an investor must carefully read its prospectus and study its historical performance and expense ratio. It is also wise to consult an advisor to determine whether a particular fund is suitable for you.

One popular technique for mutual fund investing that also uses the principle of consistency in investing is called "dollar-cost averaging."

This involves periodic investments into mutual funds at specified consistent intervals, regardless of market conditions.

By following such a consistent strategy—say, a weekly or monthly investment of a hundred dollars—you are forced to buy fewer shares than you normally would when the price per share is high, and to buy more shares than you normally would when the price is low. The result is a lower average cost per share. Consider the following example, illustrated in table 3.2:

Table 3.2 Calculating Average Share Price and Average Price per Share

MONTH	AMOUNT INVESTED	SHARE PRICE	NUMBER OF SHARES OBTAINED
1	$100	$10.00	10.000
2	$100	$9.00	11.111
3	$100	$8.00	12.500
4	$100	$7.50	13.333
5	$100	$7.00	14.286
6	$100	$6.00	16.667
7	$100	$5.50	18.182
8	$100	$5.00	20.000
9	$100	$4.00	25.000
10	$100	$3.00	33.333
11	$100	$2.00	50.000
12	$100	$1.00	100.000
	$1,200	$68.00	324.412

Average share price: $5.67
Average price per share purchased: $3.70

Study carefully the relationship between the last two columns. As you can see, as the price falls, an increasing number of shares are purchased. This is why the average price per share purchased is $3.70, not $5.67. The average price of a share is $5.67, which is obtained by dividing $68.00 by 12 (months).

$$\frac{\text{total share prices}}{12 \text{ (months)}} = \frac{\$68}{12} = \$5.67$$

The average price per share purchased is determined as follows:

$$\frac{\text{total amount invested}}{\text{total number of shares}} = \frac{\$\,1{,}200}{324.41} = \$3.70 \text{ per share}$$

The two equations give different pieces of information. The first deals with the average prices paid and the number of months it took to acquire the shares, while the second focuses on the number of shares owned and the money that was invested. What you learn from the first equation is that $5.67 is the *average price* that the shares are worth, while the second equation reveals that $3.70 is the *average cost* of those shares.

Now look again: The average price is $5.67. The average cost is $3.70. If this investment method you are forever paying the *average cost* for shares that are forever worth a higher *average price*, doesn't it suggest that this method produces a built-in-profit? Absolutely!

This is the power of dollar-cost averaging. Like diversification, it works very well—but only under certain conditions:

1. The amount of money invested must be consistent.

2. This money must be invested at regular intervals.

3. The invested money must be recently obtained (new money, not money from reinvested proceeds).

4. This system must be maintained for a long period of time (years).

Without question, your retirement plan, if you are employed, is an ideal vehicle for taking advantage of dollar-cost averaging. This is true for four reasons:

1. Your paycheck is the same amount each pay period, so you can place the same amount into your plan each time.

2. You get paid at regular intervals, so the contributions to the plan are made at regular intervals as well.

3. The money gets invested the same day you are paid, so it is "fresh cash."

4. You can expect to be working for a long time—years and probably decades. That's more than enough time for dollar-cost averaging to ride the waves of the market's volatile performance.

Whatever strategy you use, the point is to invest regularly, consistently, and without regard to a particular market level that may cloud your investment judgment. The goal is to accumulate wealth for the long term.

Faith-Based Mutual Funds

Because mutual funds offer a selected portfolio of investments, they can be designed to follow certain chosen guidelines, including those dictated by principles of faith. Faith-based funds can be not only ethical but also profitable, yielding a 10 percent annual rate of return. In fact, there are several Islamic-based mutual funds that over a long period, say, fifteen years, provide returns in excess of 10 percent. You can search for these funds on fund ranking and research sites such as Morningstar or Lipper.[11]

Most faith-based funds start their stock picking by screening out what they call "sin stocks." These are stocks in companies that produce harmful products or offer immoral services, such as abortion, pornography, gambling, alcohol, or tobacco.[12]

Jay Peroni, who specializes in faith-based investing, cautions us, however. What one denomination may think is acceptable for investment, another may not. "There are different opinions even within one faith," he says.[13] Daren Fonda, in his article "Faith and Finance" in *Smart Money* magazine, describes the criteria used by various faiths, from evangelical Christians to Mennonites to Muslims, and how they impact historically on fund performance.[14]

Today there are several mutual funds designed to meet Islamic requirements, such as Amana Income Fund (AMANX), Amana Growth Fund (AMAGX), Imam Fund (IMANX), Azzad Ethical Mid Cap Fund (ADJEX), Azzad—The Wise Capital (WISEX), and the Amana Developing World Fund (AMDWX). These funds avoid interest (riba) by not investing in bonds and other fixed-income securities. Nor do they invest in businesses that deal in goods and services considered harmful by Shari'ah law. These funds seek to offset inflation by making long-term equity investments.

Mutual funds based on Islamic principles follow several guidelines that have been agreed upon by Muslim legal scholars. These principles cover not only how the companies whose stocks are in a given portfolio should conduct business but also other aspects of the fund, including how the fund is managed. Investments following Islamic principles adhere to the following:

1. Transactions must be free of interest ("unearned income").

2. Money in itself should not be used to produce money. There should be direct participation in an economic activity.

3. Competition is encouraged, in contrast to monopoly. Eliminating monopoly is regarded as a prerequisite to justice and growth.

4. Bribery and stealing are prohibited.

5. Justice and fairness in all aspects of business transaction are required.

6. Transactions must be documented and witnessed.

7. Each person must be given his or her due share.

8. Productive enterprise, cooperation, and development must be encouraged.

9. Development efforts must include social development. Individual cooperation must be voluntary, not forced.

10. Hoarding of money is strictly prohibited. One of the purposes of zakah is to discourage hoarding (and encourage investments).

11. Unnecessary destruction of nature is prohibited, but moderate exploitation of resources is allowed.

12. Labor should be valued and must be compensated. Laborers should get their fair remuneration without delay.

13. Speculation is not allowed.

14. Harmful goods and services cannot be produced, consumed, or traded. These are the following:

   - Alcohol

   - Tobacco

   - Pork-related products

   - Unjust financial services (conventional banking, i.e., interest-based banks or savings and loan associations)

   - Weapons used to suppress people or for mass destruction

   - Immoral entertainment (casinos, gambling, pornography, etc.)

   - Illegal drugs

   - Harmful products (items that cause pain or suffering under normal use)

Amana Mutual Fund

Amana (ticker symbols: AMANX, AMAGX, and AMDWX), headquartered in Bellingham, Washington, is the first and largest US mutual fund following Islamic principles. The Amana Funds are unique in that they were specifically conceived to meet the specific needs of Muslim investors.

For example, Muslims are motivated to save and invest in order to prepare financially to make the hajj, which in Islam is considered one of life's primary duties. The money used for hajj must be saved and invested according to Shari'ah principles. To make the hajj, a Muslim must first get his or her financial house in order, which presents special challenges if the money is to be invested in compliance with Shari'ah principles.

The guidelines that Amana follows when deciding whether to buy, hold, or sell stocks are in keeping with Islamic principles. These guidelines, or screens, help Amana sift through and select potential investment opportunities.

The first factor Amana considers when buying stock is the company's debt-to-market capitalization ratio, since Amana will invest only in companies that have moderate to low debt. The debt-to-market capitalization ratio should be less than one-third.

It is understandable that companies do and will borrow money from time to time to expand business or add new equipment or undertake new ventures. However, when companies start getting into trouble, the common trend is for them to borrow more money. Four prominent examples are Enron, MCI, WorldCom, and Adelphia. The debt-to-market capitalization ratio of these four companies used to be less than one-third, then jumped higher than one-third. An investor following Amana's policy would have sold his or her stock twelve to eighteen months before these companies went down. In fact, Amana did own stock in Enron, but following its guidelines and screens, it sold off its Enron stock long before the company's devastating collapse.

The second factor Amana looks at is the company's accounts receivable and cash deposits. The acceptable ratio [(accounts receivable + cash) / total assets] is less than 45 percent. If the ratio is more than 50 percent, the company's stock can be traded but only at book value, without any premiums.

The third factor Amana considers is whether impure revenue (interest, selling pork and wine, etc.) earned by the company is less than

Table 3.3   Applying Amana Mutual Fund Screens

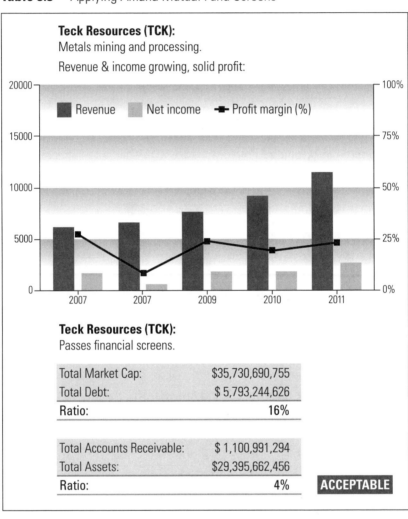

Teck Resources (TCK):
Metals mining and processing.
Revenue & income growing, solid profit:

Teck Resources (TCK):
Passes financial screens.

Total Market Cap:	$35,730,690,755
Total Debt:	$ 5,793,244,626
Ratio:	16%

Total Accounts Receivable:	$ 1,100,991,294
Total Assets:	$29,395,662,456
Ratio:	4%

ACCEPTABLE

5 percent. We find that companies who generate large income from interest and are accumulating large amounts of cash, are often are afflicted with the "urge to merge;" and may be a strong indicator that the business isn't a good investment (excess cash often indicates poor management or reinvestment deficiencies). Dividends received from such a company can be purified by giving away in charity this percentage of "impure income."

Table 3.3 shows how these financial screens are applied to a company called Teck Resources.

Amana has grown steadily over the years and is now experiencing exponential growth. A recent *MSN Money* article praised Amana and the return it was providing to investors. It also stated that, among social and religious investors, Muslims have the best chance to do well. The fact that Amana does not invest in banks that lend money based on interest or in companies that borrow heavily has helped.

Modes of Islamic Financing

One of the current trends in finance these days is the growing interest in socially responsible financing, a quest that Islam supports. Islamic finance promotes universal human improvement and, along the way, yields a fairer distribution of benefits than most conventional finance approaches. The following Islamic financial principles are being further developed and refined in various types of financial arrangements:

Mudarabah (Profit Sharing). Mudabarah is a contract under which the two parties, the supplier of capital and the entrepreneur (general partner), share the profits according to an agreed-upon profit-loss-sharing (PLS) ratio. The PLS ratio is typically 50:50 or 40:60.

The first key element of a mudarabah contract is that the financier or investor is not guaranteed a specific profit. There is no fixed annual or monthly payment. This is in direct contrast to conventional interest-based lending and financing, in which a loan is not contingent upon the profit or loss of the enterprise, requires monthly payments, and is normally secured by a collateral.

The second key element is that the financier or investor is not liable for losses beyond the capital he or she has contributed, and the entrepreneur does not share in financial losses except for the loss of his or her time and effort.

Musharakah (Joint Venture). Musharakah is a partnership contract between two or more parties, each of which contributes investment capital. The first element of a musharakah contract is that both parties contribute capital. Profits are shared by a prearranged agreement, not

Table 3.4 Comparison Between Conventional and Murabahah Transactions[1]

	CONVENTIONAL LOAN	MURABAHAH TRANSACTION
Underlying transaction	Loan (money with money)	Sale (money for goods)
Profit to bank	May be variable or fixed according to customer and bank mutual agreement	Price must be fixed
Asset for bank upon funding	Loan receivable	Sales receivable
Late payment	Additional income to bank	None or charity – because *riba al-nasi'ah* [2]
Restructuring	Yes, at additional interest	Restricted: Extension of time (loan duration) without increasing the amount due.
Early settlement	May agree to rebate formula up front and in documents	Rebate at bank's discretion
Sell portfolio to third parties	Any price – may discount	Exchangeable without premium or discount (*bai al-dayn*)[3]
Default	Continuing liability	No liability; however, a Muslim should honor its commitments

1. Copyright 2012 All Rights Reserved SHAPE™ Financial Corp. From: The CIFA Guide to Islamic Finance. Permission granted to M. Yaqub Mirza to reproduce with attribution.

2. A type of riba that exists in, or results from, a sale transaction that unduly benefits one the counterparties in the form of a surplus or extra amount due to delay of delivery of his or her side of the transaction. More specifically, riba al-nasi'ah arises in loan transactions (on the basis of future repayment of more than the principal) as well as sale transactions (on the basis of deferred price). An example of loan-based riba al-nasi'ah would be a loan with $1,000 principal on which $1,200 is to be paid

necessarily in proportion to their capital contribution. In case of loss, parties share in proportion to their capital contribution.

The second element is that all parties share in determining how the investment is managed. Thus any partner has the right to examine the enterprise's books and supervise its management. The third element is that liability is unlimited.

Murabahah. Murabahah is a cost-plus-profit margin contract whereby the financier purchases an asset on behalf of the entrepreneur and sells it, usually at a profit or higher price, to the entrepreneur at a predetermined price, paid over time. The key characteristic of a

Table 3.4 Continued

Murabahah, a sales contract with the profit disclosed to the buyer, is the main tool of modern Islamic finance. The nature of murabahah is to sell and give credit by allowing deferred payment. Because murabahah discloses the seller's price and profit, and results in credit, many global banking authorities permit it as a credit instrument.

In the United States, banks with Islamic financial products such as University Bank engages in home finance via murabahah to purchase order. Instead of lending money to the customer secured by a mortgage, University Bank buys a house selected by the customer, receives title, and then sells it to the customer. This gives the bank some risk of having to dispose of the house if the customer declines to complete the transaction, and the bank is unable to claim penalty interest for late payments. Customers who wish to have more time to pay their murabahah off will have the same price with no adjustments to raise the price. Around the world, banks use murabahah for consumer goods finance, import finance, and commercial supply programs. In some countries, banking authorities allow banks to hold inventories waiting for customers to come, select an item, which the customer may then buy on murabahah basis.

This differs from a conventional loan significantly, as a loan is an exchange of one amount of money for more money later. But, in a murabahah transaction there must be a non-monetary good or item to be sold in exchange for money. Finally, since murabahah involves goods, the buyer has many rights, which include inspection and the right to reject any goods that are faulty or not as described.

---

next year. An example of sale-based riba al-nasi'ah is a sale of 100 kg of dates to be paid back with 120 kg six months later. This type or riba is clearly forbidden in Qur'an. It existed in the pre-Islamic era in the Arabian peninsula, and thus was known as riba al-jahiliyah (riba of the era of ignorance).

3. The Arabic term for the trading of debt is *bay al-dayn*. The majority of scholars in the Middle East consider the trading of debt to be similar to trading of money. In general, this means that a debt can only be transferred at face value and not traded at market value, as many conventional bonds are.

murabahah contract is that ownership of the asset remains with the financier until all of the payments have been made. For a comparison between murabahah and conventional transactions, see table 3.4.

Ijarah (Leasing). In an *ijarah* contract, the financier purchases the asset on behalf of the entrepreneur and allows him or her to use it for a fixed rental payment. The entrepreneur may eventually opt to buy the assets at a previously agreed upon price. The key characteristic of *ijarah* is that ownership of the asset remains with the financier or is gradually transferred to the entrepreneur as the lease payments are made.

Istisna'a (Manufacturing Finance). Istisna'a is a contract of exchange with deferred delivery applied to specified made-to-order items. General principles of this practice are difficult to identify; however, very often the following are true:

- The nature and quality of the item to be delivered must be specified.

- The manufacturer must make a commitment to produce the item as described.

- The delivery date is not fixed; rather, the item is deliverable upon completion by the manufacturer.

- The contract is irrevocable after the commencement of manufacture except where delivered goods do not meet the contracted terms.

- Payment can be made in one lump sum or in installments, and at any time up to or after the time of delivery.

- The manufacturer is responsible for sourcing the inputs to the production process.

Istisna'a differs from ijara (rent or lease) in that the manufacturer must procure the raw materials. Otherwise the contract would amount to hiring the seller's wage labor, as occurs under ijara. Istisna'a also differs from *bay salam* in that (a) the subject matter of the contract is always a made-to-order item, (b) the delivery date need not be fixed in advance, (c) full advance payment is not required, and (d) the istisna'a contract can be canceled but only before the seller commences manufacture of the item.

Practically speaking, it is best to undertake a business or production of a product when one is confident it can be successfully established or completed, yet even in the most optimistic situations there is always risk. It is in this context that some instruments of lesser risk, like murabahah, ijarah, and diminishing musharakah, are allowed by Shari'ah scholars. It is also wrong to say that these instruments have an element of camouflaged interest. In fact, if implemented with all their necessary conditions, as Shari'ah scholars have always stressed, they are substantially different from interest-based financing.[15]

Qard al-hasan (Benevolence Loan). *Qard al-hasan*, a zero-return loan, or negative investment, is a great vehicle for community development. It is not a profit-making transaction; it is a social service vehicle providing an interest-free loan to an individual in need or to an organization.

Takaful (Pooled Money for Emergencies). *Takaful* is a type of Islamic insurance in which members contribute money into a pooling system in order to guarantee each other against loss or damage. It offers an alternative to conventional life, property, and car insurance. The principles of takaful are as follows:

- Policyholders cooperate among themselves for their common good.

- Every policyholder pays his or her subscription to help those who need assistance.

- Losses are divided and liabilities spread according to the community pooling system.

- Uncertainty is eliminated concerning subscription and compensation.

- No advantage is derived at the cost of others.

A Note about Insurance

Takaful is a form of cooperative or mutual insurance. Its purpose is not profit but to uphold the principle of "bear ye one another's burden." Muslims are discouraged from using the various kinds of conventional insurance because they may contain elements of uncertainty (*al-gharar*), gambling (*al-maisir*), or usury (riba).

However in 2006, the Fiqh Council of North America discussed the thirty-six-page research paper on life insurance in the United States written by Dr. Mokhar Maghraoui, one of the most respected and renowed Muslim scholars in North America, and came to the following conclusions:

- The practices and laws regulating life insurance in North America have changed significantly to allow for more equitable transactions and to prevent deceptions and uncertainty.

- The life insurance contract is a hybrid of *ta'awn* (mutuality) and *istithmar* (investment), which are both Islamically sound transactions.

- Each specific life insurance contract must be examined to see that is free of riba—that is, that no funds are invested in interest-paying instruments like bonds.

Therefore, a variable life insurance policy that allows the policy owner to allocate premiums for investment in selected equity mutual funds (preferably Shari'ah-compliant funds) is acceptable. "He [Allah] has explained to you in detail what is forbidden to you except under compulsion of necessity" (6:119).

Islamic Banking in North America

Several Islamic financial institutions have emerged in North America in the past few years that are using modes of transactions following Islamic principles. This has been made possible due to several changes in the US and Canadian regulatory environment.

The US Office of the Comptroller of the Currency (OCC), the administrator of national banks, has permitted banks to offer murabahah and ijarah to their customers.[16] Many banks, including Bank of America, Bank One (in Ohio and Michigan), Bank of Whittier (in Los Angeles), Devon Bank (in Chicago), and University Bank (in Ann Arbor), currently provide or are in the process of providing some of these financing alternatives.

University Bank

University Bank is the first bank in the United States to create an Islamic subsidiary, University Islamic Financial Corporation (UIF). University Islamic Financial is committed to running in accordance with Shari'ah principles.[18] It offers FDIC-insured mudarabah deposits to Muslim customers nationwide. It provides ijarah home and commercial financing. It also offers various forms of Islamic financing for residential and commercial properties, as well as FDIC-insured profit-sharing CDs and money market funds. The profit-sharing rates vary as the "rental" income fluctuates. They also vary based on how the underlying financed asset performs.

Having started its home finance efforts in Michigan, University Islamic Financial is expanding its home and commercial financing product into additional states, including Maryland, Virginia, Indiana, Ohio, California, New York, New Jersey, and Texas.

For individuals (primarily those who are older) not wanting to take the higher risk associated with investing in stocks or mutual funds, mudarabah is a great choice. One can also "park" funds in these accounts in between investments or while waiting to make an investment decision. University Bank hopes to expand its investment options and to offer takaful insurance to its clients and financial institutions nationwide.

4 | Pillar Four: Spending

Spending and saving are closely intertwined. Managing spending, especially daily expenses, makes it possible to save, as we saw in chapter 2. In turn, saving makes it possible to spend, especially on big-ticket items. The strategies that support success in savings, including the use of technology (such as Quicken or a simple Excel spreadsheet), are the very same strategies used for managing one's spending.

For the purposes of this book, I define spending as "spending wisely money that is earmarked for living." In a lifetime, you can save a tremendous amount of money by learning to spend wisely. Learning this skill is just as important as developing the habit of saving your hard-earned cash. In fact, it's more important, because there is no end to spending. When spending is not under control, it can negatively impact every area of your financial life.

One of the easiest ways to spend your money in a deliberate and conscious manner is to establish a personal budget—a spending plan. Planning helps to condition your thinking and shape your behavior when it comes to spending money. It teaches you to become aware of the money going out for the items vital to living (such as groceries, rent, mortgage, car payment, debt repayment, utilities) and to manage your impulses to buy things you don't necessarily need. At the same time, it allows you to plan for purchasing things you want but may not need—things that improve the quality of life, like education, owning a car or a house, and hajj. How to spend intelligently on these and similar items is the topic of this chapter.

Steps to Spending Money Wisely
The following three steps will take you well down the road toward mastering spending:

The first step is to learn to control your impulses. Especially in the United States, we're conditioned at a very early age to consume, and to consume from impulse. By conducting most of your major spending from plans and budgets, you'll begin to limit impulsive purchases.

The second step is to give yourself time before making any major purchases. Sellers of big-ticket items have made it very easy for people to make a quick purchase. A car dealer can arrange a test drive, craft an offer, and get you into an executed contract on a new vehicle within a matter of hours. The intelligent approach is to take the time necessary to properly research and evaluate your options before setting foot into the dealership.

The third step is to get in the habit of using cash or a debit card for most purchases. This habit alone can accelerate your ability to both track and control your spending. It's so easy to buy things we really can't afford by just putting it on credit, and what starts off as a small balance soon becomes a large one, taking years to pay off purchases that have long since been consumed.

Paying for a College Education

Most of us at some time face the challenge of paying for higher education, whether trying to find scholarships for ourselves or helping a loved one achieve his or her academic goals. Not only have educational standards greatly changed recently, but professions have become more specialized, meaning that students now need a higher degree—perhaps a master's degree or specialized training—just to land their first job.

As student loans are becoming more difficult to obtain, carefully planning to save for college has become crucial. Assuming the person going to college is not yet eighteen, these investments should be made in an Education Savings Account (ESA, discussed in the next section).

Anyone who has met my father can probably attest to his devotion to saving and efficiency. Almost every day, my dad shares a new way he found to save: a new website, a new way of doing something ordinary, or simply utilizing some restraint. Even savings of a couple of pennies were retold as major victories. My father's devotion to saving—and efficiency—was trumped only by his belief in education and personal improvement.

While we had to plead and bargain for movies and videos, anything that could be described as "educational" Abba would buy without hesitation. My first cell phone was couched in the terms of allowing me to attend more school events and extra-credit assignments, since I'd be able to arrange for rides and it would allow my mother to contact me at all times, and therefore raise my grades (all for only an extra $10 a month!). Of course, that was before the bill for excessive text messaging arrived. Now that was harder to explain!

By always being willing to spend his hard-earned and -saved money on educational activities, both scholastic and religious ones, my dad engrained in me the importance of education and self-improvement. The opportunities they provided and allowed access to warrant their cost. While saving money was important, that saved money was meant to better our lives or the lives of those around us.

—Sana Y. Mirza, Ph.D. Candidate

You can use the following worksheet (table 4.1) to determine the approximate amount of money that should be saved. The table includes an example: The family of Fatima, currently age eight, plans that, in ten years, she will attend a university that currently charges $6,000 per year. This means that the family needs to invest $2,220 annually (e.g., $555 quarterly or $185 monthly) in an ESA account to pay the entire tuition.

Alternatively, Fatima's parents can open an ESA account for the child by making a gift of $2,000 and next year contribute another $2,000. Even if they add nothing more to the account, by age 18, Fatima will have about $13,000 toward her college education from that initial investment of $4,000. Of course, additional contributions will make the fund grow even larger.

These figures are based on the assumption that university education costs will rise at the average rate of 3 percent per year (due to inflation) and that the expected pretax average return on investment will be 8 percent per year. Tables 4.2 and 4.3 show the inflation rate and the investment factor calculated for eighteen years.

Here is another example of calculating the amount of money to save for college, starting when the child is one year of age:

Child's age	= 1 year
Years to college	= 17 years
Estimated cost	= $6,000 per year
Estimated cost for 4 years of college in 17 years	= $39,600
Yearly investment	= $1,173
Quarterly investment	= $293
Monthly investment	= $97

Wouldn't it be nice to be able to pay for items we want (or need) to buy without debt? The same tables and worksheet can be used to plan for a wedding, hajj, buying a car, making a down payment on a house, acquiring a business, vacations, retirement, or any other major expense. Here are some additional examples:

Table 4.1 Worksheet for Financial Planning for Higher Education

EXPECTED COST OF COLLEGE EDUCATION

SCHEDULE A: Expected Cost of College Education

		FATIMA	YOUR CHILD
1.	Current age of the child	8	
2.	Years to college (18 minus child's age)	10	
3.	The current cost of a college education (in-state) (in 2011, approximately $6,000 per year)	$6,000	
4.	Inflation factor (from Table 4.2) corresponding to number of years in line 2 above	1.34	
5.	Multiply line 3 by line 4 above to find the estimated future cost of college education at the end of the number of years specified in line 2	$ 8,040	
6.	Future total cost for four years of college	$32,160	

HOW MUCH SHOULD BE INVESTED

SCHEDULE B: Lump Sum Investment

		FATIMA	YOUR CHILD
1.	Enter amount from line 6 in Schedule A	$32,160	
2.	Enter lump sum return factor from Table 4.3	2.16	
3.	Divide line 1 by line 2 to find lump sum investment now	$14,900	

SCHEDULE C: Periodic Investment

		FATIMA	YOUR CHILD
1.	Enter amount from line 6 in Schedule A	$32,160	
2.	Enter periodic return factor from Table 4.3	14.50	
3.	Divide line 1 by line 2 to find the annual target amount	$2,220	
4.	Divide line 3 by 4 to find the quarterly target amount	$555	
5.	Divide line 3 by 12 to find the monthly target amount	$185	

Table 4.2   Inflation Factor

(Assuming that the cost is rising due to inflation at an average of 3 percent per year)

YEARS TO EXPENDITURE	INFLATION FACTOR	YEARS TO EXPENDITURE	INFLATION FACTOR
1	1.03	10	1.34
2	1.06	11	1.38
3	1.09	12	1.42
4	1.12	13	1.47
5	1.16	14	1.51
6	1.19	15	1.56
7	1.23	16	1.60
8	1.26	17	1.65
9	1.30	18	1.70

Table 4.3   Investment Factor

(Assuming a pretax average return of 8 percent per year)

YEARS TO EXPENDITURE	LUMP SUM	PERIODIC YEARLY	YEARS TO EXPENDITURE	LUMP SUM	PERIODIC YEARLY
1	1.08	1.00	10	2.16	14.50
2	1.17	2.08	11	2.33	16.66
3	1.26	3.25	12	2.51	18.99
4	1.36	4.51	13	2.71	21.51
5	1.47	5.87	14	2.92	24.23
6	1.59	7.34	15	3.15	27.16
7	1.72	8.92	16	3.40	30.33
8	1.86	10.64	17	3.67	33.75
9	2.00	12.50	18	3.96	37.45

Car

Buy a reasonable used car now, and save enough money to buy a good one later. Or, if the car is bought and financed today, your payment would be approximately $466 per month.

Average cost (2013) = $20,000
Years to purchase   = 5
Cost in 5 years   = $23,760
Yearly investment   = $4,752 (perhaps investing your tax refund)
Monthly investment = $396

Wedding

Average Cost (2012) = $15,000
Years to marriage   = 4
Cost in 4 years   = $16,800
Yearly savings   = $3,725 (perhaps investing your tax refund)
Monthly investment = $310

Perhaps this is the only way to pay for the cost of a wedding, as I do not know of any institution that will finance it.

Opening an Education Savings Account

One way to deal with higher education costs is to open an Education Savings Account (ESA) or a Section 529 college savings plan. Both can be wonderful college savings devices due to their tax advantages. However, while a particular state's 529 plan may be a good tool to save for college, most of these plans do not offer investment choices. You simply participate in an established program with set investment options that may or may not be suitable for people of certain faiths, such as Muslims.

An ESA account, on the other hand, is similar to an IRA account, where funds can be invested according to one's wishes. It can also be a self-directed account, which allows the individual to make an annual nondeductible contribution to a specific trust account, where the funds grow free of taxes. There is also no tax when the money is withdrawn, as long as the funds are used for education and educational materials.

An ESA is surprisingly easy to set up. The first step is to figure out who is eligible for an ESA. The beneficiary must be under the age of eighteen during the period when the contributions are being made.

Second, the amount to be contributed has to be determined. The contributors, if filing their taxes jointly, must have a modified adjusted gross income of less than $190,000—or less than $95,000 for single filers—to qualify for the full $2,000 deduction. For incomes up to $220,000 ($110,000 for single filers) smaller contributions can be made.

Third, where to establish the ESA must be decided. Any bank, mutual fund, or other financial institution can serve as a custodian. Although there is no limit to the number of ESAs that can be established for a child, the combined contribution from multiple givers may not exceed $2,000 per year per child. This presents a great opportunity to save for the education of your child or grandchild, or even for the child of a friend or of a needy person).

In summary, the benefits of an ESA (as of this writing) are the following:

- The maximum annual contribution to an ESA remains $2,000 per child (under 18 years of age).

- Withdrawals for kindergarten through college expenses are not taxed.

- Hope and lifetime learning tax credits can be claimed during the same tax year when tax-free ESA withdrawals are made to cover education expenses.

Those who do not qualify to set up an ESA may establish and contribute to a regular savings account (or UGMA account, under the Uniform Gifts to Minors Act). It is also possible to establish both kinds of accounts with no limitation—though giving more than the gift tax exclusion (in 2014, $14,000) per year per child may be subject to a gift tax).

A UGMA account, which is a custodial account, offers a bit of tax relief. Income and capital gains of up to $850 are untaxed, while the next $850 is taxed at the child's rate (generally 15 percent and subject to kiddie tax rules).

A custodial account belongs to the child; an adult controls it until the child is eighteen. After that, the child is free to spend it as he or she wishes.[1] The advantage of an ESA in this regard is that it can be used only for educational purposes (with a UGMA the eighteen-year-old may decide to buy a BMW rather than get an MBA!).

By establishing an ESA, you can help a child fulfill the obligation of seeking knowledge. The Qur'an states: "O my Lord, advance me in knowledge" (20:114). If the child does not attend college, the ESA can be used for someone else. There are no adverse tax consequences, as long as the funds are used for educational purposes.

In the Muslim community we are often invited to many *aqeeqa* (parties to introduce newborn children). Instead of taking the usual kinds of gifts, consider giving the parents of the newborn a check in the name of an Islamic mutual fund, and tell them to open an ESA for the baby, after studying the prospectus carefully, of course. Few gifts are better than the gift of education.

As an example, Inayah was born on March 4, 2007. Her grandparents were so excited to have their first grandchild, they kept asking themselves what they could do for her that would have a positive effect on her life forever. They decided to give her the gift of education by depositing $2,000 in an ESA through an Islamic mutual fund investing in growth stocks. On her first birthday they gave her another gift of $2,000 sent to her ESA.

In May 2009, Inayah's aunt, Asma, was graduating with her MBA and wanted to use her own ESA to pay her tuition. However, the value of her account was low because the stock market had taken a plunge in March 2009. Instead of liquidating her ESA at a loss, she decided to gift it to her niece. That way, it would remain invested, and when the market recovered, the ESA's market value would be higher again. So Asma transferred her ESA ($3,724) to Inayah.

Inayah's grandparents also gifted her with $2,000 on her third, fourth, fifth, and sixth birthdays. So now her ESA account has grown to $24,157.

On her eighteenth birthday, depending on stock performance and with no additional contributions, Inayah stands to have approximately $62,800 in her ESA. If, in addition, her parents start contributing

$2,000 per year until she is eighteen, she will have approximately $120,000. (See Table 4.1 to make these calculations.)

Once she is eighteen, Inayah may be able to extend these funds even further. By taking advanced placement courses, she may get her bachelor's degree in three years instead of the usual four. In this case she would have enough money to go to any school she wants—public or private—without incurring debt. She'll avoid having student loans to pay for the rest of her life!

If Inayah spends less on her education by getting a scholarship or attending a good public university, she has enough money in her ESA. Excess funds can be used for earning her master's degree, or she can gift leftover ESA money to her siblings or cousins (as did her aunt).

Planning for the Hajj

Islam prescribes that all financially and physically capable Muslims perform a pilgrimage to Mecca—the hajj—once in a lifetime. Besides commanding his Companions to perform the hajj, the Prophet Muhammad taught them the way the hajj rituals were to be performed. He also advised them on how to prepare for the hajj, financially and otherwise. The Prophet raised the religious and ethical value of pilgrimage so high that it became the ultimate worldly hope and crowning event of every Muslim's life.

The hajj is the purest self-presentation before God. It should be undertaken as a response to God's calling. The phrase that the pilgrim chants throughout the pilgrimage (*Labbayk Allahumma*—I am here, O Allah!) is an expression of this acquiescence to Allah's call.

Muslims prepare for the hajj as if they were leaving this world forever. That is why many write their wills before starting on this journey. First, they have to pay off their debts, including any zakah due on their wealth. They return whatever was given to them in trust. They rely on their savings to pay the expenses of the journey, such as airline tickets, hajj tax, lodging, and the sacrifice of an animal. In addition, they have to provide for their families and dependents during their absence. They must have earned and saved enough to cover those expenses. No hajj is valid if performed "on credit."

Every Muslim must make hajj a priority and plan to perform it at least once in his or her lifetime, as soon as possible. In the opinion of some, the cost of performing hajj a second time may be better spent if it is contributed to Islamic charities.

What is the cost of hajj for someone living in the United States? How much should be invested? Let us assume hajj costs rise an average 3 percent per year, due to inflation, with a pretax average investment return of 8 percent per year. Taxes to be paid on investment income should also be accounted for.

The accompanying worksheet for hajj financial planning (table 4.4) can help you determine the amount to be invested. For example, if a person plans to perform pilgrimage in five years, assuming hajj costs $5,000 per person today, then the person needs to put aside and invest a lump sum of $4,300 or else invest either $1,100 annually, $275 quarterly, or $92 monthly. The intending pilgrim may consider investing more than these amounts to cover for rising costs or a lower investment return. For a husband and wife, simply multiply these amounts by two.

Purchasing a House

Few people are able to purchase a house outright, paying cash. However, because conventional mortgages involve interest, they are not *halal*, or permissible, under Islamic law. This problem has been addressed in several ways.

In 1975, a group of Muslims in Halifax, Nova Scotia, Canada, bought a home and implemented a precursor to today's interest-free housing financing (see below), including shared equity and rental terms. That particular home was paid off in three years. Today, interest-free housing is still unusual in the West, where property is customarily purchased through a conventional mortgage.

Almost at the same time, a group of Muslims in Plainfield, Indiana, organized the Indiana Housing Cooperative. Several people purchased their homes through this co-op. In this type of business partnership, shareholders (partners and/or investors) invest money in a single home and rent it to one of the partners. The renter is allowed to buy back the shares from other owners to increase his or her ownership

Table 4.4   Worksheet for Hajj Financial Planning

EXPECTED COST OF HAJJ
SCHEDULE A: Cost of Hajj

1. Number of years from now when you plan to make hajj $ _____
   (*insha Allah*)

2. The current cost of hajj per person (in 2011, about $5,000) $ _____

3. Enter inflation factor (from Table 4.2) corresponding to $ _____
   number of years in line 1 above.

4. Multiply line 2 by line 3 above to find the estimated future $ _____
   cost of hajj at the end of the number of years you specified
   in line 1.

HOW MUCH SHOULD BE INVESTED
SCHEDULE B: Lump Sum Investment

1. Enter amount from line 4 in Schedule A. $ _____

2. Enter lump sum return factor from Table 4.3. $ _____

3. Divide line 1 by line 2 to determine the lump sum $ _____
   investment required.

SCHEDULE C: Periodic Investment

1. Enter amount from line 4 in Schedule A. $ _____

2. Enter periodic return factor from Table 4.2. $ _____

3. Divide line 1 by line 2 to find annual target amount. $ _____

4. Divide line 3 by 4 to find quarterly target amount. $ _____

5. Divide line 3 by 12 to find monthly target amount. $ _____

and eventually buy the property. Property values and appreciation determine share and rental amounts.

In 1982, when interest rates in the United States and Canada rose to almost 20 percent, many people, including Muslims, lost their homes. Consequently, the idea of a shared-equity rental (SER) was revived,[2] catching the attention of the Canadian Broadcasting Corporation.

Later, a successful housing cooperative in Toronto financed hundreds of homes.

Currently there are several housing cooperatives operating in the United States and Canada. However, by the very nature of cooperatives, which involve investments only from members and other individuals (who often have limited finance resources), the cooperative model can support just a limited number of homebuyers at any given time. Additionally, cooperatives are "illiquid," meaning their securities are not freely traded on the financial markets and there is no secondary market where securities of the cooperative can be traded (i.e., bought and sold).

Another solution to the problem of purchasing a house without interest has been the development of interest-free home financing. In order to respond to the growing needs of Islamic home financing, Guidance Financial, a licensed mortgage lender, came into the market. Later, because of their ability to sell a nearly unlimited number of mortgages to Fannie Mae and Freddie Mac, several banks, such as Devon Bank, La Riba affiliate, Bank of Whittier, Broadway Bank, and United Trust, began offering interest-free home financing.[3]

Then, in December 2005, University Bank formed the first Islamic banking subsidiary, University Islamic Financial (UIF), which is currently the only US bank that offers Islamic financing for residential and commercial properties using Islamically acceptable documentation. Freddie Mac agreed to accept this documentation without any modification or promissory note. This provided cash in the secondary market for these securities, resulting in UIF's having the capacity to provide an almost unlimited number of financings. Its home financing and deposit products are backed by a fatwa from leading Islamic scholars. It is also able to service the financed transactions after origination in an Islamically acceptable format.

If you would like to help someone (a relative, child, or grandchild), give them a one-time gift (up to the current gift tax exclusion). If invested (Islamically) for, say, seven years, the recipient may have about $29,000. Supplemented with his or her own savings, the total will make a nice sum for the down payment on the purchase of a home.

A Roth-IRA: An Individual Retirement Account

A Roth-IRA (an investment account provided by most banks and mutual funds) is a great way to save for retirement. The funds grow tax-free, and upon retirement (or after age 59½) of the investor, withdrawals (principle plus accumulated growth) are all tax-free. Five years after a Roth-IRA account is opened, the principal contributed can be withdrawn.

If you want to help someone who is good and hard-working but for one reason or another has not been able to save for his or her retirement, you can encourage that person to open a Roth-IRA account with an Islamic mutual fund (that invests in growth stocks) and gift that person, in the form of contributions to the Roth-IRA, $4,000 annually.[4] The recipient will certainly thank you.

I know a couple who set up such an arrangement for several relatives. One of these relatives, Noor, now age fifty, has approximately $33,000 in her Roth-IRA. Assuming no more contributions are made, and using the calculation for the inflation factor provided in table 4.2 and figuring a rate of return of 10 percent, at age sixty-seven she is likely to have $151,700. This is enough to supplement her social security income.[5] However, if she can contribute even small amounts to this Roth-IRA herself, she will have even more funds to enjoy at her retirement.

As Noor approaches retirement, she may want to consider rolling over part of these funds into a profit-sharing CD that matures at staggered dates over a period of time, say, one year, two years, and five years.[6]

Gifting and the Gift Tax

In the United States, an individual can gift up to the dollar amount of the gift tax exclusion (in 2014, $14,000) per year per person without paying the gift tax. You may choose to gift a portion of this amount, say, up $5,000, to a Roth-IRA for your children, your siblings, relatives, friends, or anyone you like in the community (provided the person earns at least that much during that year and his or her adjusted gross income is less than $105,000). The remainder of the amount (in this example, $9,000, figuring a gift tax exclusion of $14,000) can be gifted for investment in a mutual fund (preferably one following Islamic principles). This money is available for use whenever the need arises.

You also can give the following without triggering the annual gift tax exclusion rule:

- Gifts to a spouse

- Gifts to a charitable organization (these gifts are tax-deductible)

- Gifts of educational expenses. These are unlimited as long as you make a direct payment to the educational institution for tuition only. Books, supplies, and living expenses do not qualify.

- Gifts of medical expenses. These, too, are unlimited as long as they are paid directly to the medical facility.

5 | Pillar Five: Giving

"Help yourself by helping others. Those who do good, do well."
– Sir John Templeton

All the great faith traditions require and encourage giving. Giving is the essence of living. It touches everything we do that is truly meaningful. I believe we are all here to make a difference—otherwise what is the purpose of living? As we live and experience the world during our time here, our contributions hopefully leave the world a better place. We also give to provide cross-generational fairness; that is, if we are doing well, then let us do something so the next generation will have the same opportunities.

Giving is not meant to encourage dependency in the receiver or create a permanent underclass. Most of us support the principle: it is better to teach a man how to fish than to give him a fish. However, by serving those genuinely in need, we are serving God Himself. This is said on multiple occasions in the Qur'an as well as in the Jewish Bible and the Christian New Testament:

> And don't forget to do good and to share with those in need. These are the sacrifices that please God. (Hebrews 13:16)

> And spend of your substance in the cause of Allah, and make not your own hands contribute to [your] destruction; but do good; for Allah loves those who do good. (Q 2:195)

> Those who spend [in charity] of their goods by night and by day, in secret and in public, have their reward with their Lord: on them shall be no fear, nor shall they grieve. (Q 2:274)

> For I was hungry and you gave me something to eat, I was thirsty and you gave me something to drink, I was a stranger and you invited me in, I needed clothes and you clothed me, I was sick and you looked after me, I was in prison and you came to visit me. (Matthew 25:35–36)

> You will be made rich in every way so that you can be generous on every occasion. (2 Corinthians 9:11)

> You shall open your hand to your brother, to your poor and needy in your land. (Deuteronomy 15:11)

A person who cannot give money should give whatever he or she has available to give, as illustrated in the following two stories:

> The Prophet Muhammad said: "Every Muslim has to give in charity." The people then asked: "[But what] if someone has nothing to give, what should he do?" The Prophet replied: "He should work with his hands and benefit himself and also give in charity [from what he earns]." The people further asked: "If he cannot do [even] that?" The Prophet said finally: "Then he should perform good deeds and keep away from evil deeds, and that will be regarded as charitable deeds."[1]

> The Prophet Muhammad said: "Charity is prescribed for each descendant of Adam every day the sun rises." He was then asked:

"From what do we give charity every day?" The Prophet answered: "The doors of goodness are many . . . enjoining good, forbidding evil, removing harm from the road, listening to the deaf, leading the blind, guiding one to the object of his need, hurrying with the strength of one's legs to one in sorrow who is asking for help, and supporting the feeble with the strength of one's arms—all of these are charity prescribed for you." He also said: "Your smile for your brother is charity."[2]

In Islam, giving falls into two categories: obligatory giving, called zakah, and voluntary giving, known as sadaqah. These are discussed in the remainder of this chapter.

The Prophet said, "God, whose Majesty and Glory are but manifest, has enjoined a portion for the poor in the wealth of the rich that is within their capacity [to give]. If they withhold it from them until they go hungry, naked, or their lives become a continuous hardship, God shall be severe in holding them accountable for what they had done and punishment shall be stern" (narrated by Ali ibn Abi Talib).

In light of the aforementioned statements, I often wonder about the significance of the various percentages of zakah ("portion" of wealth prescribed) on different sources of wealth—what do these various percentages really mean?

I recognize that many Muslims distribute their zakah directly to individuals or charitable organizations of their choice; therefore, estimating total zakah that is being given out (by a community as a whole) is nearly impossible.[3] However, I made a very rough estimate that faith-based community centers like those found among Muslim communities (and in the other Abrahamic faiths) often receive perhaps 10 percent of the zakah that is actually due of that community.

But I am an optimist at heart. I feel that, if every Muslim (and person of faith) calculates his or her zakah (tithe) accurately—based on the prescribed percentage(s)—and faithfully distributes it on a consistent basis, then we should be able to totally eliminate poverty from the world.

If this was not to happen, the Creator might have chosen higher percentages, so that poverty would be eliminated and everyone would live with dignity! In fact, it has been historically documented that we once lived in a time when Muslims, when seeking to pay zakah, could not find anyone who qualified to receive the tithe.

Understanding Zakah

For those who have money to give, Islamic law requires that they give it on a yearly basis as zakah (charity, or wealth tax). Zakah is considered so important that it is the third of the five pillars of Islamic faith.

Fulfillment of this pillar requires Muslims to reach out to the community and to interact with others in a meaningful and profound way. Just imagine, how would you know if someone is in debt? Is that person going to approach us and say, "I have $17,000 in credit card debt?" Probably not. However we may come to know this as we become actively involved in the community and exchanges of personal information occur. Then we can know who is in need of receiving zakah.

Zakah is similar to tithing in Jewish and Christian traditions. The words in Hebrew (*ma'aser*) and in Greek (*apodekatoo*) for "tithe" both simply mean "a tenth." The Hebrew Bible says one should tithe 10 percent of what one earns:

> "For every tenth part of herd or flock, whatever passes under the rod, the tenth one shall be holy to the Lord." (Leviticus 27:33)

> "and this stone that I have set up as a pillar will be God's house, and of all that you give me I will give you a tenth." (Genesis 28:22)

In the New Testament the actual percentage required is unclear. It simply suggests tithing "in keeping with your income" (I Corinthians). Some churches use the 10 percent figure stated in the Jewish scripture as a general guideline or "recommended minimum."

> "Woe to you, teachers of the law and Pharisees, you hypocrites! You give a tenth of your spices—mint, dill and cumin. But you have neglected the more important matters of the law—justice, mercy and faithfulness. You should have practiced the latter, without neglecting the former" (Matthew 23:23).

Zakah as the obligation to the needy is decreed by God, the ultimate Owner and Giver. The Prophet used to give whatever exceeded his needs, placing his faith in God to provide: "They ask how much they are to spend; Say: Whatever is beyond your needs"' (Q 2:219). M. Umer Chapra comments: "The prescription of zakah is a clear and unambiguous signal of the Divine desire to assure that no one suffers because of lack of means to acquire the essential need-fulfilling goods and services."[4]

Zakah means "purification, growth, blessing, and appreciation." Funds on which zakah has not been paid are "impure," polluted. But giving a percentage of those funds as zakah purifies them.

Zakah is based on the Qur'anic injunction: "Take alms from their wealth so that you might purify and sanctify them" (Q 9:103). In other words, giving a stipulated percentage of wealth, or a voluntary un-stipulated amount, purifies the owner of that wealth from stinginess, greed, meanness, lack of sympathy with the needy, and similar feelings. Prophet Muhammad said: "Those who give zakah from their property [will find that] their sins will leave them." The Qur'an says that zakah will give satisfaction and reward in both worlds (Q 61:10–11), whereas impure wealth will bring suffering and punishment in this world and the hereafter (Q 3:180). One hadith states, "People who do not pay zakah will suffer, in disaster, famine, or drought."[5]

The Qur'an also says: "O ye who believe! Give of the good things which ye have [honorably] earned, and of the fruits of the earth which we have produced for you, and do not even aim at getting anything which is bad, in order that out of it you may give away something, when you yourselves would not receive it except with closed eyes. And know that God is free of all wants, and worthy of all praise" (Q 2:267).

Who Deserves to Receive Zakah?

The Qur'an (Q 9:60) specifies eight categories of those who are entitled to zakah:[6] the poor, the needy (destitute), zakah administrators, those whose hearts are to be reconciled, captives (those held in bondage), debtors, wayfarers (those who are stranded), and those receiving it in the cause of Allah. All but the last category are defined. The last category is broad enough to include any kind of community welfare. Thus, Islamic community centers can receive zakah because they promote moral values and act as *da'wah* (propagation of faith) centers. The Prophet allowed zakah to be used for education, for promoting religious causes, and for strengthening the *ummah* (community).

The Qur'an makes clear that zakah is meant to help the hard-working poor who are in need but do not beg, in contrast to those who beg for a living and do not work hard. The modest poor take precedence in receiving zakah. It must be stressed that the people who deserve zakah most are not beggars, especially since many of them adopt begging as a profession, but rather those whose modesty prevents them from asking for help. The Prophet emphasized that "a needy person is one who is modest." And the Qur'an teaches, "Charity is for those in need, who, in Allah's cause are restricted [from travel], and cannot move about in the land, seeking [for trade or work]: the ignorant man thinks, because of their modesty, that they are free from want. Thou shalt know them by their [Unfailing] mark: They beg not importunately from all the sundry" (Q 2:273).

Dr. Muhammad Ali al-Hashimi comments: "The purpose of zakah is not to give the poor person a few dirhams[7] to keep him going, rather the purpose is to help this poor person attain a suitable and dignified standard of living, one that is befitting to man whom Allah has honoured and appointed as His viceregent on earth, without either extravagance or stinginess."[8]

Regarding refugees, caring for them and giving zakah to help with their basic necessities is highly recommended. Many of them fall within the categories of "poor," "needy," "under debt," or "wayfarer," and "in the cause of Allah." They are implicitly included in the verse on who should receive zakah, says Shaikh Taha J. Al-Alwani, former chairman of the Fiqh Council of North America.[9]

For example, after the invasion of Kuwait in 1990, many well-to-do fled (most likely in their expensive cars) to Saudi Arabia, where they had nothing to live on: no money, no shelter, no clothing, and no resident visa. The locals used zakah to help meet these "wayfarers'" needs. Can Muslims in the United States do the same? The answer is yes.

You may be wondering: What about the IRS? Can we give to a refugee who does not have legal status? Benson Tesdahl, a specialist on tax-exempt law, says yes. "There is no obligation I have ever seen imposed by the IRS or the courts that would require a charity to check the immigration status of a poor or needy person. Any number of charities across the country running soup kitchens and other programs . . . I don't know of any who check the immigration status of the recipients. Obviously, it would be impractical for the government to require [it], and there would be a general uproar if the government were to impose such a rule."[10]

Shaikh Yusuf al-Qaradawi, in his *Fiqh al-Zakah: A Comparative Study*, explains: "Zakah does not aim only to improve the state of the totally deprived and financially broken, but is also for those who find they can't fully meet their basic needs." He also says, with regard to giving zakah to students: "Full-time students are eligible for zakah. Students may be given zakah in order to help them achieve that purpose, including cost of necessary books, regardless of whether the knowledge sought is secular or religious."[11]

Muslims may also give charity to people of other faiths. As Abu Saud says, There is no text in the Qur'an or Sunnah that prohibits giving non-Muslims zakah. If one is poor, needy, a wayfarer, or employed to administer zakah, whether Muslim or non-Muslim, they are eligible for zakah (as long as they are not fighting against Islam and Muslims).[12]

The Qur'an says, "God forbids you not, with regard to those who don't fight you for [your] faith, nor drive you out of your homes, from dealing kindly and justly with them: For God loves those who are just" (Q 60:8). This verse was revealed for those Muslims who hesitated to give charity to their unbelieving relatives.

In another verse, we are instructed, "And they feed, for the love of Allah, the indigent, the orphan, and the captive" (76:8). "Captives" in Muslim society were usually unbelievers, as reported by al-Hasan and others, says al-Qaradawi.

Similarly, Ibn Abbas says, "They (the Companions) used to dislike giving charity to their kin and relatives who were unbelievers. They asked and were permitted to do so by this verse: 'You are not responsible for their guidance, but God guides whoever He wills. Whatever good you give away is to your own benefit, when you give desiring only the Face of God. Whatever good you give away will be repaid to you in full. You will not be wronged." (Q 2:272)[13] According to Ibn Kathir, this verse means that if the giver of charity aims to please God, he or she will be rewarded by God regardless of whether the recipient of charity is righteous or not, deserving or not. The giver is rewarded for his or her intention.

M. Umer Chapra's comments on giving and receiving zakah include references to several Qur'an verses:

> The payment of zakah by the rich is not a favour to the poor. The rich are not the real owners of their wealth; they are only trustees (Q 57:7). They must spend it in accordance with the terms of the trust, one of the most important of which is fulfilling the needs of the poor. Any attempt on the part of the rich to show it as a favour, thus injuring the feelings of the poor, reflects their insincerity and destroys their reward in the Hereafter (Q 2:261–74). The poor should also not treat the receipt of zakah as a personal disgrace because what they are receiving is only their right ordained by God in the wealth of the rich (Q 51:91 and 70:25). They are, moreover, free to choose how to spend their receipts of zakah. It is their money and they may spend it in accordance with their own priorities, which would, in a Muslim society, be within the constraints of the Shari'ah. However, anyone who can provide for himself and does not deserve to receive zakah but still does so, will be disgraced on the Day of Judgement because he is in essence guilty of acquiring income wrongfully and of violating the rights of others. There may not, therefore, be any need for an elaborate system of means testing which tends to be demanding, expensive, time-consuming, and inconvenient. It would nevertheless be wise, at least in the initial phase, to be alert to misuse and indiscriminate handling of funds. The informal social control system present in a morally charged Muslim society would help weed out violators. By effectively eliminating those who are able to take care of themselves, the system should be able to provide meaningful assistance to those who are really needy.[14]

Limit of Exemption (*nisab*)

Whether a person should give or receive zakah, and also the amount a person should give, are determined by his or her level of wealth. The "minimum amount of wealth subject to zakah" is known as *nisab*.[15] Nisab is based on the amount of wealth or income that a family needs to live a simple but decent life for one year.

Nisab encompasses essential commodities and services, such as food, clothing, dwelling, education, medications, vehicles, and the tools of a trade or profession. Thus nisab is an accurate and equitable basis for determining a limit of sufficiency. The limit of sufficiency differs from one community to another and according to family size. Nisab is thus similar to the "consumer's basket." It also parallels in some ways the poverty index for a specific locality in the United States.

Anyone whose income is less than the nisab is entitled to zakah. Anyone whose income is more than the nisab must pay zakah.

When to Pay Zakah

Zakah is paid annually by all Muslims whose wealth is above a specific amount, and is to be spent for the public welfare. Donors can give more, but never less, than what is due, and cheating in the calculation of zakah is a sin punishable under Islamic law.

No zakah is due on wealth held for less than one year. Muhammad's wife 'Aishah related that the Prophet said, "No zakah is due on wealth till one (full) year passes."[16] Since a complete fiscal lunar year must elapse when a person's assets reach nisab, each individual will have a different zakah year.

Zakah is calculated on the basis of the lunar year cycle, which is shorter than the Gregorian calendar by eleven days, so an investor using a Gregorian calendar has to adjust the zakah amount accordingly. This means that the 2.5 percent zakah due on certain kinds of income is actually 2.58 percent, and the 10 percent zakah due on other kinds of income is actually 10.3 percent.

Zakah can be paid any time. Many prefer to pay it during the month of Ramadan or Rajab, while some prefer to pay zakah during Muharram, the start of the Hijri year. As long as nisab is reached during a given year, most jurists agree that zakah can be paid in advance of the end of the calculated zakah year, or whenever there is an urgent need such as during a flood, earthquake, or recession.

An estimated monthly zakah payment is highly recommended, for this helps to spread the payments over a period of time, and it fulfills zakah's purpose sooner rather than later. The final calculation and reconciliation of payments, however, can be done at the end of each lunar year. Or for your convenience, you can calculate zakah every calendar year's end (December 31), when all your financial information for the year (W-2, 1099, K-1, etc.) is available and you are working on your tax return.

After death, unpaid zakah is deducted from the inheritance after all debts are settled.

Delaying zakah without reason beyond a short period is not permissible, because you are holding funds that belong to those entitled to receive them. Qaradawi says, "The significance of zakah distribution is detailed in the Qur'an: It is essential that the proceeds of zakah be distributed and not kept in the state treasury (as was done before Islam by emperors and kings with the levies they imposed on their subjects)."

In the Qur'an we are told to "pay the rightful dues that are proper on the day that the harvest is gathered" (Q 6:141) and "race to do good deeds" (Q 2:148). The Prophet said, "The best of good deeds is the one done promptly," and, "The action most loved by Allah is the one which *endures*—even though it be small."[17]

Calculating Zakah

Zakah is due on the current year's gross income before taxes—zakah, the right of Allah, is calculated before the rights of man (taxes).[18] Zakah is also due on savings and investments that their owner has held for one lunar year, all stocks in trade above the nisab, and real estate and capital goods if they are owned (not kept on credit) and stocked for trade (not production).

The wealth from which zakah is paid excludes debts and such liabilities as a home (and its contents essential for living), jewelry that is customarily used, land, buildings, and capital materials used in or for production.

Uninvested capital is subject to a 2.5 percent zakah per year—which means that the zakah payments on this wealth, if not invested, would make it disappear in about 30 years. This is one reason Islamic teachings encourage Muslims to invest in productive enterprises. Besides producing more money for the owners than the 2.5 percent zakah payment, investing money in businesses adds to society's wealth and creates jobs. Zakah also adds to economic health by circulating wealth and helping to eradicate poverty. The Prophet said, "Wealth shall never decrease as a result of charity (sadaqah)."[19]

Zakah paid to a charity is tax-deductible. To maximize this tax-deduction, you may want to pay zakah by contributing appreciated assets (calculated at the appreciated fair market value), so no capital gains taxes have to be paid. However, Dr. Muzammil Siddiqi, a former president of the Islamic Society of North America (INSA), advises that any money you retain when you reduce federal and state taxes should be added to the next year's income and is subject to zakah at that time.[20]

Shaikh Yusuf al-Qaradawi explains how to calculate zakah: "The rate of 2.5 percent due on assets whose zakah is calculated on the principal and its increments together once every year (on items such as livestock and trade goods). Regarding the harvest, a rate of 10 percent is due (calculated based on crops and produce at harvest time), when land is irrigated by rain or spring and 5 percent is due in the case where land is irrigated by man. The asset may be materially fixed, such as land, or non-fixed, such as bees."[21]

The 10 percent for harvest and 5 percent if the crops are grown on irrigated land are based upon the words of the Prophet. The Prophet said, "In whatever [plantation] irrigated by rain or springs or reached water by itself, the due zakah is one-tenth. And in whatever irrigated by an instrument the dues are half the one-tenth." A similar hadith reports that the Prophet said, "In whatever rivers and clouds [rain] irrigate, tithes are due and in whatever is irrigated by instrument, half the tithes [is due]."

Some jurists suggest that rented houses, buildings, and factories should be treated like trade goods, appraised yearly, and subjected to a 2.5 percent zakah on the appraisal value. However, from a practical point of view, the required yearly appraisal is cumbersome, subjective, and requires the services (and cost) of specialists. Others calculate zakah on the income from such assets—assuming the nisab is reached.

Qaradawi says that zakah can be taken from the asset's revenue. He concludes that zakah on rented buildings and fixed industrial assets is taken out of their income—not the principal—at the rate of 5 or 10 percent. Zakah is calculated on net income at the rate of 10 percent when net income after deducting costs can be calculated, as is the case with corporations. This approach is based on the fact that the Prophet levied 10 percent zakah on crops irrigated by rain or natural springs, as if he were taking it from the net produce.

Qaradawi further concludes that shares of purely industrial and nontrade (i.e., manufacturing) corporations, such as those dealing with refrigeration, hotels, advertising, public transport, shipping, and airlines, are not subject to zakah, since their capital (represented by shares) is invested in machinery, offices, and buildings, which are not subject to zakah. However, he says that 10 percent zakah should be levied on dividends and then on capital gains realized upon sale (if any).

Cash and Cash Equivalents

Passive investments (e.g., cash, coins, gold, certificates of deposit, guaranteed bank credits, money market accounts, and bonds), require 2.5 percent zakah payment on the principal plus any yield on funds invested for a lunar year (2.58 percent per Gregorian year).

Fixed income instruments, such as bonds, are not recommended investments according to Islamic law. However, the fact that interest is prohibited does not exempt someone receiving interest from payments from zakah (which is 2.5 percent per year on principal and interest income). One who indulges in the forbidden must not be given any privilege.

Risk Investments: Shares and Mutual Funds

Zakah is due on the profit—not on the amount invested—in publicly traded stocks (listed on a stock exchange or included in a mutual fund). These are considered "active" investments, for they are investments in commercial, industrial, and development (real estate) businesses. In this case, zakah is 10 percent of the net realized profit (i.e., total return) on funds invested for a lunar year (10.3 percent per Gregorian year).

For simplicity's sake, and to share the returns with others sooner rather than later, it is advisable to consider the portfolio's market value at the beginning and end of each calendar year (including dividends realized and unrealized gain/loss), minus new investments and plus withdrawals and/or redemptions, and then pay 10.3 percent of that year's appreciation (total return). If there is no appreciation, no zakah is due. The portfolio's market value at the end of the calendar year is its beginning value for the following year.

Shares of private corporations and general/limited partnership interests can also be considered "active" investments. Since their market value is not readily available, the zakah is 10.3 percent on only the dividends or distribution received, and on realized gains, if any, upon sale of the partnership's interest.

For additional information and detailed illustrations on zakah calculations, please refer to the following section of the Amana Mutual fund website: www.amanafunds.com/retail, then select "Zakah" from the main menu.

Buildings, Factories, and Businesses (Nontrading)

The owner of a business or rental property can determine net income after deducting costs, such as labor costs, utilities, maintenance, taxes, and debt service. Depreciation/amortization is also considered a cost. (It accumulates enough reserve funds to acquire a new asset at the end of the old one's productive life.) However, to calculate profit from a personal business, a factory, or rental property for zakah purposes, one must add all reserves (capital reserves, bad debt reserves, and contingencies) to the distributed profit. Both Qaradawi and Abu-Saud say that zakah is 10.3 percent per Gregorian year on the net pretax profit (as calculated above) from a building, factory, or business, assuming the nisab is reached.

Stock Options and Stock Purchase Plans

Stock options and employee stock purchase plans are granted by companies to attract and retain the best available personnel for important position, and to provide incentives for employees, consultants, and outside directors. Stock options may be ISOs (incentive stock options) for employees or NSOs (nonqualified stock options) for nonemployees. The stock option holder is entitled to purchase a specified number of corporate stocks, vesting over a number of years (usually five years), at a certain price (usually the stock's fair market price on the day the grant is made). The grant, therefore, has no immediate cash value. However, over time, the option's value may increase or decrease as the underlying stock price changes.

There are two usual ways to cash in on this wealth. The first is to regard it as a same-day sale, meaning the option holder exercises the option to buy stock and then sell the stock on the same day. In this case, the realized gain is treated as additional income for that year. Zakah on earned income is 2.58 percent per Gregorian year, minus nisab.

The second way is to exercise and hold the stock, meaning that the option holder exercises the option to buy the stock and then holds onto it as an investment. Zakah is 10.3 percent on the gain, which is the sale price minus the exercise price, when the stock is eventually sold.

Employee stock purchase plans allow employees to purchase stock from the employer, usually at a discount, for example, 85 percent of the market price. Upon sale, the zakah rate is 10.3 percent on the net gain, which is the sale price minus the purchase price and any sales commission.

There is no zakah due at the time of a stock option grant or when the stocks are acquired through the stock purchase plan. Zakah is due when the stocks are sold at a profit, at which point a zakah of 10.3 percent of the profit or gain is due, subject to nisab.

Retirement Accounts, Life Insurance Policies, and Annuities

Contributions to retirement accounts (unless made after paying zakah) and subsequent growth in these accounts are subject to zakah, as the contributor has access to these funds, especially the vested portion, and may dispose of them at will (although it may be subject to penalty and taxes). Therefore, if your 401(k), Keogh plan, IRA, SEP-IRA, or Roth-IRA is invested in a stock portfolio, you may pay 10.3 percent of the yearly increase in the portfolio's value.

Contributions to retirement accounts made after zakah is paid on income for that year are excluded from the calculation of zakah. Also, investments held for less than a year are excluded.

A 10.3 percent per year zakah is due on the increase in cash value of a life insurance policy, annuities, and other investments held in a personal trust, provided these investments are made in stocks or active business. Otherwise, cash in a life insurance policy, annuity, or other passive investment is treated as cash or cash equivalent, so zakah of 2.58 percent per year is payable on the principal plus any increase in value during the year. If these accounts are converted to an annuity that pays a monthly sum to meet daily expenses over a specified period or for life, the periodic payments should be treated as income subject to 2.58 percent per year, preferably payable monthly after deducting nisab.

Stocks received as compensation or as a bonus are part of earned income; therefore they should be added to the income for that year. Zakah on earned income, minus nisab, is 2.58 percent per Gregorian year.

Telling People How Much Zakah to Pay

Even at age eleven, I understood that establishing one of the first faith-based mutual funds [the Amana Mutual Fund] was no easy feat. I tried to sit still and carefully listen to the presentation about market share and services. Afterwards, I tugged on my dad's shirt and asked, "Daddy? Do you have to pay zakah on this investment? If so, can you tell people how much they need to pay and then they can give it to poor people?"

The next thing I knew, I was repeating my idea to his business associates. They smiled and said, "If your Daddy can teach us how, we can write the computer program to calculate zakah." True to their word, within a few years, zakah calculation and resources became a standard service for all of the fund's clients.

—Asma Y. Mirza, MBA

Public trusts and charitable organizations are not subject to zakah.

To help you determine the proper amount of zakah, I have enclosed a calculation form from the Foundation for Appropriate and Immediate Temporary Help (FAITH) (see table 5.1).[22] Feel free to reproduce it and share it freely with others.

Giving While Living

A man came to the Prophet and asked, "O Allah's Apostle! Which charity is the most superior in reward?" He replied, "The charity which you practice while you are healthy, niggardly [miserly] and afraid of poverty and wish to become wealthy. Do not delay it to the time of approaching death and then say, 'Give so much to such and such, and so much to such and such.' And it has already belonged to such and such [as it is too late]." [23]

Following this Hadith, I strongly argue for giving while living. Why? Giving while living provides you with an opportunity to see the effects of your gift. While living, you can direct or redirect the use of your contributions. If a project you contributed to does not succeed, you have the opportunity to contribute to another one.

Imagine what would happen if no one gave while living—if everyone only willed, upon death, a portion of their wealth (up to one-third of their estate, according to Islamic law) to the poor or needy and noninheritors. The recipients would be praying for the person's death, waiting to receive the charity to fulfill their needs! Instead, during one's lifetime, once the loved ones are provided for and zakah has been paid, one should give back (sadaqah) to the community.

Abu Sa'id al-Khudri reported God's Messenger as saying, "It is better for a man to give a dirham as sadaqah (charity) during his lifetime, than to give a hundred at the time of his death." [24]

You may ask: "Is it better to leave for a child a trust account or a great society?"

Gifts can be made in favor of a living person capable of holding property. However, unless you use your lifetime exemption, under IRS rules, gifts per person per year that exceed the gift tax exemption ($14,000 in 2014) are subject to the gift tax. On the other hand, unlimited personal gifts can be made to a mosque, a community center, a school, or any charitable institution (as well to your spouse, provided your spouse is a US citizen).

I am encouraged by the growing number of people worldwide who are embracing the notion of giving while living. I see this as a reflection of the best qualities contained with the act of sadaqah, and it's my hope that this trend in giving and contribution continues to grow—through your lifetime, your children's lifetime, and beyond.

While most examples of this trend—as covered by the media—mostly reflect the actions of the world's richest individuals, there is a more interesting—and all-inclusive—trend that makes giving while living accessible to a broader range of people. With the advent of the internet, social-media platforms, and concepts such as crowdsourcing (like kiva.org), it's now easier than ever for people with modest resources to make contributions that, when pooled, can have a positive impact on the society.

For those of you who wish to explore giving while living, the Atlantic Philanthropies has come up with a simple nine-step process to help you in your quest. You can access this process along with other materials on giving while living from their website: www.atlanticphilanthropies.org.

"Giving while living" is not a uniquely Muslim or Islamic concept.[25] Andrew Carnegie, in his famous 1889 essay, "The Gospel of Wealth," argued that the wealthy have a duty to give back and help their communities during their lifetime, and not merely in death. He strongly referred to those who mainly give away wealth after death: "Men who leave vast sums in this way may fairly be thought men who would not have left it at all, had they been able to take it with them."[26]

It is an obligation on the wealthy to support their communities and to focus on giving back while living. We also know that the Prophet taught that giving charity would not in any way decrease our wealth.

Donor-Advised Fund (DAF)

Giving can be accomplished through a will or by paying zakah and sadaqah, perhaps to a donor-advised fund (DAF). A donor-advised fund is essentially a "foundation within a foundation," and a low-cost alternative to a private "personal" foundation.

Contributions made to a DAF are irrevocable and unconditional. Contributed assets become the fund's property and cannot be returned to the donor under any circumstances. For contributions to be a completed gift, the Charitable Gift Account allows donors to recommend—but not control—grants.

However, by contributing to a DAF you are able to maximize tax savings without having to immediately decide where your gift will go. You may donate to the fund over time or in a lump sum all at once, while maintaining the flexibility to recommend where the funds will be applied at a later date.

With a donor-advised fund, the donor's requests are considered; however, the fund's trustees, as fiduciary, have discretion regarding grant recipients.

A DAF can be used to help establish a *waqf* (an endowment—a *sadaqah jaria*, a continuous charity, in which the principal is never touched and only income is used for charitable purposes) at a lower cost and with possibly greater tax benefits than a private foundation. The profits can be used for education, scholarships, community activities, or charitable purposes. Generally, charities as defined in Section 501(c)(3) of the Internal Revenue Code can be beneficiaries of such grants.

Wealthy individuals can create sizeable endowments under Section 501(c)(3) by establishing private or publicly supported tax-exempt trusts or foundations engaged in religious, charitable, scientific, literary, or educational work. In general, an endowment provides cross-generational fairness, that is, it helps future generations to have a chance to succeed. Individuals and corporations can deduct from their taxes contributions of cash or appreciated assets (e.g., stocks, real property, etc.) with some limitations, made to tax-exempt organizations.

The Qur'an encourages Muslims to give in charity: "The parable of those who spend their wealth in the way of God is [that of] a grain of corn: it grows seven ears and each ear has a hundred grains. God gives manifold increase to whom He pleases: and God cares for all and He knows all things" (Q 2:261). "But whoever believes, and works righteousness—he shall have a goodly reward" (Q 18:88).

Charitable Remainder Trust (CRT)

With a charitable remainder trust (CRT), assets (property or money) are donated to the CRT while the donor continues to use the property and/or receive income from it while living. The donor receives the income, and the charity receives the principal (after a specified period of time, or upon the death of the donor.) The donor does not have to pay any capital gains tax on the donated appreciated assets and also gets an income tax deduction for the fair market value of the remainder interest donated to the CRT. In addition, the asset is removed from the estate, reducing subsequent estate taxes.

While the contribution is irrevocable, the donor may have some control over the way the assets are invested. The donor may even switch the ultimate beneficiary—that is, the named charity—to another charity, as long as the new charity is a qualified charitable organization.

This is a win-win situation for the donor and the charity. For example, if a seventy-year-old donor with assets valued at $100,000 (which may have been originally purchased for $25,000) donates through a CRT, he or she receives an income of $5,000 per year for life. For this donation, he or she receives a tax deduction of about $60,310 (equivalent to a total savings in taxes of about $18,000, considering 30 percent federal and state tax) and pays no capital gains tax on this appreciated asset, which is donated to the CRT. Upon the person's death, the charity gets the asset.

Whether or not to use any of these charitable giving vehicles depends upon each potential donor's individual circumstances. Consultation with the appropriate advisors is highly recommended.

Family Foundation

A family foundation is a legal entity whose purpose is to fulfill the family's wishes and vision by giving charitable grants and gifts for designated purposes from its own funds and investment earnings. As defined in Internal Revenue Code Section 501(c)3, the foundation can give to charities in the United States and elsewhere for charitable, educational, scientific, literary, and/or religious purposes, as well as other activities as may be desirable or required to accomplish the foregoing objectives and purposes. The foundation may not engage in nonexempt activities, such as political campaigns and events.

Here is an example of a family foundation: In 2008, our family decided to form a family foundation in order to create a vehicle to give back to the community and to continue the family's legacy. Through the foundation we invest in specific projects that align with our family's approach to philanthropy. The foundation does not consider unsolicited requests for grants.

My wife and I plan to help our children to purchase their homes, with the understanding that when they are in a position to do so, they will give the same amount to our family foundation. After learning about this, our daughter Asma remarked: "This is a great deal." When I asked her why, she replied: "Well, there is no due date and no interest (or rent sharing), and when you pay back you get a tax deduction!" We are sure that our children and their spouses will continue the tradition of giving, and there are additional incentives that make it even more exciting.

The primary reason to form any kind of foundation is to do good and to create a stream of money for charitable purposes that may continue into perpetuity. This is a *sadaqah jariyah*, a perpetual charity, that keeps on giving, for which the donor receives God's rewards even after death. Creating a foundation is like planting palm trees to provide shade and fruit, even though those who plant them may never get to eat their fruits.

There are additional reasons to form a foundation, such as income- and estate-tax savings, getting your entire family involved in charitable work, and possibly providing income for those who do the foundation's work. Oftentimes, people establish foundations to focus their charitable goals. They may want to give back to the community in the form of scholarships or health care or helping the poor and needy, or to offer thankfulness for being blessed with a good, prosperous life.

A foundation can provide financial support to various kinds of organizations, such as the following:

- *Community organizations*: community centers, mosques, playgrounds, hospitals

- *Educational organizations*: schools, colleges, libraries, scholarship funds, dormitories

- *Social-services organizations*: shelters for the elderly, orphanages, low-income housing projects, prisoner rehabilitation centers, half-way housing projects, debt-relief societies

Islam and Money

I think that a classic example of our relationship to both Islam and money is characterized in the various projects Ammi (mother) got us involved in to raise funds for the masjid. Each and every one of those projects involved a lot of hard work and sacrifice of our time and energy, and none of them resulted in financial compensation or too much recognition. [Our parents] taught us that we shouldn't expect compensation when we were "giving for the sake of Allah (swt).*"

They also taught us that the money that we were raising was sacred in some way because we had to be very careful with this *amaana* (trust) that we were holding on to, because it didn't belong to us, it belonged to God.

My father was incredibly careful about being honest and not taking favors for several reasons: (1) you don't want to feel indebted to others, (2) we shouldn't take advantage of people's generosity, (3) the organization's money is an amaana (trust) that we were responsible for and would answer for to Allah (swt), and, an extension of this, (4) multiple relationships with an organization have to be carefully monitored so that things are always 100 percent transparent and honest.

—Fatima Y. Mirza, Ph.D. candidate

Subhanahu wa ta'ala, "Glory to Him, the Exalted."

Table 5.1   Zakah Calculation Form

Schedule 1
Items Subject to 2.58%* on Income and Assets

1. Any cash on hand kept for one Gregorian year $ _____

2. Annual earned income before any deductions of taxes, $ _____
    social security, etc.

3. Value of jewelry kept for a year that is in excess of $ _____
    what is customarily used

    ADD LINES 1, 2, and 3. $ _____

4. **Less pro-rata *Nisab*** (please see example below) $ _____

5. **Income subject to Zakah** $ _____

6. Multiply line 5 by 2.58%. $ _____

    SCHEDULE 1 ZAKAH DUE $ _____

Schedule 2
Items Subject to 10.3%* Zakah on Yield

1. Realized capital gain on sales of stocks and mutual funds $ _____
    and the like

2. Dividends and rents from real estate, less expenses of debt $ _____
    and any other direct expenses, but not depreciation or reserves
    or taxes

3. The profits of shares in partnership, before deducting any $ _____
    depreciation or reserves or taxes

4. The net profit (revenue minus direct expenses such as wages, $ _____
    maintenance, taxes, debts, etc. and not considering reserves)
    of trade, business or rented property

    ADD LINES 1 through 4. $ _____

5. **Less pro-rata *Nisab*** (please see example below) $ _____

6. **Income subject to Zakah** $ _____

7. Multiply line 6 by 10.3%. $ _____

    SCHEDULE 2 ZAKAH DUE $ _____

ZAKAH DUE (Add schedule 1 and 2.)   **TOTAL: $** _____

---

* Gregorian year is 11 days longer than lunar year; hence the adjusted rates are
  2.58% (rather than 2.5%) and 10.3% (rather than 10%) per year.

Table 5.1 Continued

REMARK: If the income subject to zakah is composed of items subject to 2.58% (schedule 1) and others whose yield is subject to 10.3% (schedule 2), nisab has to be divided in the same proportion of the two items. The nisab proportion is subtracted from each category, and the result is to be multiplied by the related rate, 2.58% or 10.3%.

EXAMPLE:

Total income from Schedule 1, subject to 2.58%	$50,000
Total income from Schedule 2, subject to 10.3%	$10,000
TOTAL YEARLY INCOME	**$60,000**

For a family/household size of 5

Nisab (Poverty Limit) = $27,000 to be divided into $22,500 and $4,500. Thus

Zakah on Schedule (1) = $50,000 – (50,000–22,500) = 27,500 x 2.58%	$710
Zakah on Schedule (2) = $10,00 – 4,500 = $5,500 x 10.3%	$567
TOTAL ZAKAH DUE	**$1,277**

Combined Zakah

Total Zakah (due for the year)	$	_____
Less Zakah already paid (during the year)	$	_____
ZAKAH DUE	$	_____

Hanafis say any delay in paying Zakah which is due (now owed to others), without valid reason, even for a day or two is sinful and not permitted.

Please send your tax-deductible Zakah contribution to:

FAITH
795 Center Street, Suite 2
Herndon, VA 20170 USA
www.faithus.org
Ph: (571) 323-2198

2012 Poverty Income Guidelines

HOUSEHOLD SIZE	ANNUAL INCOME Gregorian Year (up to)
1	11,170
2	15,130
3	19,090
4	23,050
5	27,000
6	30,970
7	34,930
8	38,890
9	42,850
10	46,810

6 | Key Wealth-Building and Wealth-Preserving Strategies

"If you can't measure it, it doesn't exist."–Anonymous

This chapter discusses some of the basic strategies for building and preserving the wealth you have earned, saved, and invested. These strategies can support and supplement your efforts with the five pillars of prosperity.

In building your financial future, a long-term, consistent approach is very important. Fundamental to this approach is determining your financial goals and charting out a plan to reach them. The following is an example of how to think through and establish financial goals. You can adapt this thinking to suit your own situation and goals.

I want to use my wealth to do the following:

Buy a car

Buy a house

Put kids through college

Go on pilgrimage (hajj)

Buy a business

Retire comfortably

Help others

To accomplish these purposes my short-term goals are the following:

Accumulate one year's worth of savings to go on pilgrimage

Accumulate three years' worth of savings to purchase a car

Accumulate five years' worth of savings for a down payment on a house

My long-term goals are the following:

>   Accumulate $15,000 savings in eight years to help a child with college

>   Accumulate twenty years' worth of savings for a comfortable retirement

My strategies for building wealth are the following:

>   Save each month

>   Budget to save and invest

>   Invest and use compound returns

>   Invest in a house

>   Fully use tax-deferred investments: IRA, SEP-IRA, 401(K) plan, education IRA

My strategies for controlling debt are the following:

>   Set debt-management goals

>   Avoid accumulating debt

>   Pay off any debt I have quickly

Growing Your Assets

When you want to build a sizable estate, you should start early. In fact, you should start today. The sooner you invest, the sooner your money can start to grow.

You do not need a lot of money to start. Many mutual funds, including Amana Mutual Fund (www.amanafunds.com), allow you to start an account with as little as $250. You may also open a brokerage account if you have enough money to make investments of your choice.

It is best to open an investment account that is separate from your checking and savings accounts. This allows you to follow your investment money and also reduces the temptation to spend it. Once the account is open, you can add money on a regular basis—at least 10 percent of your paycheck, suggest Brian Ingram and Virginia Morris in *Guide to Understanding Islamic Investing.*[1]

There are two great ways to invest. One way is to buy things of value whose value you expect to increase over time, such as real estate, stocks, art, or collectibles (a growth investment). Another way is to buy things that you expect will provide regular income, for example, in the form of rents or dividends.

When you are deciding to make an investment, the following factors should be considered:

- The rate of return for investing in stocks averages 10 percent over periods of fifteen years or longer. (I know of funds that have averaged returns of over 11% per year.)

- After inflation, expected annual rates of return are around 7 percent for stocks, 2 percent for long-term bonds, and 0.5 percent for T-bills.

- While the effect of taxes is to reduce your income, the effect of tax breaks (deductions) is to let you keep more of your income.

- The longer the investment period ("time horizon"), the better the expected results ("higher investment return"). This is a compelling reason to start saving early for education, hajj, and retirement. If you want to retire early, you may have to pass on that Porsche in favor of a Toyota.

- Diversification is an excellent strategy, especially if you are in midcareer. Do not risk all your extra dollars in one kind of stock or one type of investment. Invest in stocks in different industry groups and stocks with varying potentials for growth and return. A mutual fund may be a good choice.

- Reduce risk by investing a portion of your funds in a profit-sharing money market account or in CDs (certificates of deposit) offered by banks such as University Bank (www.university-bank.com).

- Your asset allocation should take into account factors like age, cash reserves, health, income, career, and other familial needs.

What kind of investor are you? It depends on your tolerance level. Conservative (low risk) investors want to safeguard their current assets and minimize the chance of losing any invested money (principal). Moderate investors seek growth (which is higher risk) from a substantial portion of their portfolio while investing the balance to protect their principal and gain income (which is lower risk). Aggressive (high risk) investors increase their risk of losing principal in exchange for significant growth.[2]

Wealth Preservation Strategies

Perhaps equally as important as building wealth is establishing the means to preserve that wealth both during one's lifetime and after death. There are numerous ways of achieving this—too numerous to discuss at length here. What follows are the basic methods that should be considered.

A major aspect of preserving wealth is knowing how to preserve it after one's death for descendents and other beneficiaries. Thus having some familiarity with inheritance laws, both religious and secular, is useful. This is particularly true for Muslims, since Islam has specific laws about inheritance.

Inheritance Laws

Among the three religions of the book, Islam may have the most to say about rules of inheritance. Judaism also has a considerable number of inheritance laws, many of them complex. However, the basic laws of inheritance within the Jewish community are described in Numbers 27:5–11.[3]

Christianity does not have detailed inheritance laws. Geoffrey St. Marie writes: "As Christianity is subject to many denominations, there is no legal authority which covers inheritance for all Christians, other than those statements found in scripture. Instead, focus on the idea of inheritance within Christianity is of a spiritual character."[4]

In the Gospels, Jesus addresses the issue of inheritance on one particular occasion (Luke, 12:13-59). When asked by a man how he was to divide his wealth, Jesus responds by condemning earthly wealth as a fleeting phenomenon and of little concern compared to the well-being of the soul. This has caused some Christian thinkers to assert that Christianity has no laws of inheritance, since such laws would govern material affairs (money), not spiritual affairs. The prevalent concept of inheritance in Christianity, then, pertains not to earthly property but to a spiritual inheritance stemming from Abraham to Jesus. This inheritance is believed by Christians to be exemplified by the death of Jesus and his resurrection: a promise of eternal life for believers.

Islam spells out specific rules of inheritance (*irth* or *mirath*) that apply to all Muslim men and women. Every Muslim must follow the rules of inheritance unless the heirs voluntarily give up their rights to the inheritance.

The rules of inheritance are specified by the Qur'an and *sunnah* (the way of life prescribed as normative for Muslims on the basis of the teachings and practices of Muhammad and of the Qur'an). While living, Muslims are free to give to whomever they want. After death, everything must be given out according to the schedule of distribution outlined in the Qur'an.

The rules of inheritance are mentioned in several places in the Qur'an. For example, there are "settled portions ordained by Allah; and Allah is All-knowing, All-Wise" (Q 4:11–14). There are shares for ascendants, descendants, and other family members (Q 2:180, 2:240; 4:7–9, 4:11–12, 4:33, 4:176; 5:106–108). The Qur'an also encourages the sharing of wealth with the needy (Q 4:8–9).

Islamic law ensures a wide distribution of inherited wealth throughout society. M. Umer Chapra says,

> Islam has instituted a unique inheritance system designed to bring about a more equitable and wide distribution of wealth. The rules for inheritance are defined by the Shari'ah on the basis of its socio-economic objectives. No one can deprive a genuine Shari inheritor except when he is an apostate or guilty of murdering the deceased. Again, no one can make a will for more than one-third of his estate. This one-third has to be for charitable objectives or for persons not already entitled to a share in the estate (unless the other heirs agree).[5]

The Prophet said, "A man or woman may worship Allah for sixty years, but when their death comes they hurt someone in the will and thus entitle themselves for the punishment in hell."[6]

All outstanding loans or debts, taxes, unpaid dowry (*mahr*), atonement (*kaffarah*), and money for one year's maintenance for the widow and the residence must be paid before wealth is distributed (Q 2: 240). In the will a person may give up to one-third of his or her wealth to a person (or persons) who is a noninheritor or to one or more charities. The Prophet allowed a person who insisted on giving virtually all his wealth to the poor to bequeath only one-third of his wealth to them, thus establishing the upper limit of what one can give via a will to noninheritors. At least two-thirds was to be left for the dependents. The Prophet said, "Leaving your dependents well off is better than leaving them poor as they are looking up not to the mercy of others. Every expenditure which you expend on your dependents is a sadaqah (charitable expenditure), and therefore meritorious."[7]

The remaining estate must be distributed to inheritors according to Shari'ah. All shares are distributed according to the specific percentages defined in the Qur'an. Administrators should keep in mind the following:

- Only a Muslim can inherit from a Muslim. Non-Muslim relatives cannot inherit from Muslims and vice versa. If a Muslim has a non-Muslim spouse (such as a Jewish or Christian wife), he may will up to one-third of the estate to his non-Muslim spouse. A non-Muslim may accept something as a gift from a Muslim but not as an inheritance right. On the other hand, many prominent scholars such as Dr. Kamli take into consideration *maqasidi* (higher intent or purpose), where he concludes that "many prominent Companions permitted that a 'Muslim may inherit from his non-Muslim relative and vice versa' (as the Prophet himself had allowed this in some cases), as long as the non-Muslim relative is not engaged in active hostility with Muslims. Muslims to inherit from their non-Muslim relatives would encourage conversion (converting to Islam should not result in loss of inheritance)."[8]

- According to fiqh opinion, illegitimate or adopted children cannot inherit.

- A murderer does not inherit.

In the United States, most states protect heirs, especially the spouse and children, from being disinherited through a will. For instance: if the husband dies leaving a will that gives his wife only 12.5 percent of his estate, within six months the wife may choose to bypass the will and take a statutory amount known as her "elective share." In Virginia, for example, the elective share is calculated as one-third or one-half of the "augmented estate," depending on whether the deceased has surviving children or grandchildren.[9]

Notably, these legal statutes pertain only to probate law and property that passes under a will. They do not pertain to property passing under a trust (such as a living trust), or something in joint tenancy, or where a designated beneficiary is named—as with life insurance, a 401(k), an IRA, or a POD (payable upon delivery) or TOD (transfer on death) account. The probate court protects a surviving spouse from being "defrauded" by the other spouse. However, with the popularity of nonprobate assets and the use of trusts, such protections do not cover all situations.

Common Questions about Islamic Inheritance Law

The Qur'anic rules about distribution of inheritance are clear and cannot be disputed. However, once in a while, questions are raised about one or another rule. One such question is: Why does the wife receive only a one-eighth share, while his son receives twice the amount that his daughter will receive in inheritance? To understand this rule, it must be looked at within the framework of Islamic law and not in isolation. For example: should anyone feel that the wife needs a place to stay after her husband's death, while in good health he could gift a house (and anything else, for that matter) to her. Inheritance laws and distribution schedules are applied only after death.

Mazen Hashem, professor of political science at the University of Southern California, has pointed out that a girl who receives *mahr* (a marriage gift given by her husband as a required part of the marriage contract)[10] and invests it over time is better off than a boy, who receives no dowry.

In addition, a female owns and controls not only her mahr but also her inheritance and her lifetime earnings (which can be substantial). She has no obligation to pay for her living expenses; that is her husband's responsibility. Upon the death of her husband, that responsibility is transferred to her children, her siblings, and other members of the extended family. Thus the wife has other assets she can rely upon. The son has more responsibilities than a daughter, entitling him to a higher share of the inheritance.

There appears to be a lot of confusion within the Muslim community on the distribution of wealth among one's children. To begin with, while living, we must treat all of our children equally in every respect (i.e., upbringing, clothing, education, cars, marriage, and travel), and without discrimination between male and female. A child, whether male or female, has a right to sustenance, education, proper care, and being treated equally while the parents are alive. (An exception is if one child is handicapped and has special needs.) This principle is supported by Hadith. "The Prophet asked, 'Have you other children besides this one?' He said, 'Yes.' The Prophet asked, 'Have you awarded a gift like this to all of them.' He said, 'No.' The Prophet said, 'I am not going to bear witness to this act of injustice.'"[11]

The Prophet also said, "It is obligatory for a father to treat all his children equally, especially in the matter of giving gifts."[12] This Hadith is also advanced by those scholars in support of their contention that if a person wants to distribute his property among his children during his lifetime, he should not make any discrimination among his male and female children and should give an equal share to all of them. "Each one of you is a caretaker (ra'iy), and is responsible for those under his care. Wasting the sustenance of his dependents is sufficient sin for man."[13]

While you are living, you can freely give equally among your children, irrespective of their gender. It is only upon one's death that the Shari'ah schedule of distribution applies.

While living, we may want to give to charity, or give to deserving noninheritors, and distribute the rest equally to our children, leaving little to nothing for the inheritance.

Also, if a person wants to give more than one-third of the inheritance to noninheritors or to a charity (or charities) of his or her choice, he or she can do so after getting consent from the inheritors. A child with special needs can also be taken care of this way. Additionally, an inheritor can gift or forego his or her share in favor of someone else.

Wills

Everyone who is at least eighteen years old should have a will.[15] If you do not have a will, the state you live in has one for you. However, you may not like how this state-determined will divides your assets and how it selects a guardian for your children if they are underage. Moreover, the way the state law says a person's wealth should be distributed may not be according to the Islamic distribution schedule. However, every state will recognize a properly written and executed will, if it exists.

It is especially crucial that a will be written by parents of young children. If both parents pass away, if there is no will, the court will appoint a guardian over the children—quite possibly a person they did not even know and maybe of another faith. The wealth of a deceased single person without a will may go to government institutions that may serve purposes not consistent with the person's beliefs.

The Qur'an says, "It is prescribed for you, when one of you approacheth death, if he leave wealth, that he bequeath unto parents and near relatives in kindness. [This is] a duty for all those who ward off [evil]" (Q 2:180; see also 2:181–2 and 4:12). The Prophet said, "It is not right for a Muslim who has property to bequeath, that he should pass two nights without having a Will."[16]

The purpose of a will is to distribute assets after one's death in an orderly fashion to inheritors, including gifts to individuals or to one or more charities. When you write your will, keep in mind the following:

- You, the testator (the person making the will), must be at least eighteen years old and of sound mind.

- You must be able to differentiate between good and bad. Otherwise the will is not valid.

- The executor is a person appointed to carry out the provisions and directions in the testator's will.

- A guardian is a person or persons legally placed in charge of the affairs of the testator's minor children.

- The will allows you to will but not to negate willing. Thus one cannot will to disinherit a child.

- A will can be oral or written. However, under most state laws, a will must be in writing. It must be signed before a notary public and in the presence of two or three adult witnesses (depending on the state's requirements), present at the same time, who will see and sign in the conscious presence of the testator.

- The testator must sign willingly. The signature must be free and voluntary (not coerced by a family member, friend, or lawyer).

- No particular language is necessary to constitute a valid will. It can be handwritten. However, using the primary language of the country—in this case, in English—is preferred.

- The testator can revoke, change, or replace the will before he or she is on his or her death bed.

- The will should be kept in a safe place. For a small fee, the original can be deposited with the county court clerk or with probate court. Also, leave a copy with your lawyer and with the administrator of your will.

As mentioned earlier, in Islam, up to one-third of the net estate can be willed to noninheritors, i.e., relatives, nonrelatives, and charities, after all liabilities have been paid (i.e., debt, unpaid dowry (mahr), unpaid zakah, taxes, and maintenance payments for one year for the widow and residence).[17] The Qur'an says: "If any of you die and leave widows, make a bequest for them: a year's maintenance and no expulsion from their homes [for that time]. But if they leave of their own accord, you will not be blamed for what they may reasonably choose to do with themselves: God is the Almighty, the Wise" (Q 2:240).

The person making the will should be intending to do good and not to deprive anyone of his or her due rights, while obeying Allah.

Estate Planning Mistakes to Avoid

Writing a will and planning an estate are complex, detailed processes, and it is easy to make mistakes that can be regretted later. The following eight points, based on Herbert Nass's book, *The 101 Biggest Estate Planning Mistakes*, are key mistakes that can easily be avoided.[18]

1. *Dying without a will.* As discussed earlier, in the absence of a will, the court will appoint an administrator to administer your estate. If you die and leave behind young children, the court will appoint a guardian for them. The administrator and the guardian appointed by the court may not always make decisions according to your faith requirements. Distribution of your estate will be governed by the statutes of the state you live in, which most likely will not follow Islamic prescriptions. By not having a will, you are giving up your rights. Someone else will decide for you. It may also result in additional expenses (such as taxes and legal fees), not to mention aggravation and delays in the distribution of your estate.

2. *Improper execution of the will.* The will must be properly executed—not in a rush while you are leaving for umrah or hajj or when you are making an overseas trip. Proper execution of a will requires two or three (depending on your state) witnesses and a notary public. All witnesses must be present and see you sign your will according to state requirements; otherwise the will can be rejected and probate may be refused.[19]

3. *Not properly documenting the delivery of a gift.* To avoid this problem, physically take possession of the gift with a deed of gift, a written instrument that is signed and delivered by the donor to the donee (recipient) of the gift.

4. *Not specifying lease termination.* If you own rental property, add the following clause to the lease: "Lease will terminate on reasonable terms after the death of the owner of the property." This will allow the administrator of your will to sign a new lease or sell the property.

5. *Owning property in other countries.* According to Herbert Nass, it is probably a mistake to own real estate or residential property in another country, since it can cause numerous problems for the executor, administrator, and/or beneficiaries of your estate.

6. *Not discussing the will with your spouse.* Discuss the contents of your will with your spouse, since he or she may be the executor of your will. If your spouse does not like the contents, he or she may not implement them!

7. *Removing the staples.* DO NOT REMOVE staples from an original will. Photocopy the will with the staples. If you have to remove the staples, get an affidavit from the person who removed the staples, explaining the presence of the staple holes.

8. *Not properly protecting your document(s).* Do not keep your original will in a safe deposit box. Very often, after a person dies, the safe deposit box is sealed by the bank until someone is appointed the executor of the will. A person cannot be appointed executor of a will without having a copy of the will in hand. Perhaps the best place to keep your will is with your attorney or a government official, such as the county clerk.

Revocable Living Trusts

Why should someone establish a revocable living trust? Without a revocable living trust, the estate may have to go through probate proceedings, which could be costly and may prevent inheritors from receiving assets, or a decision on assets, in a timely manner. Instead, consider transferring ownership of your assets to a revocable living trust while you are alive. A revocable living trust is like a *wakf al-ahli* (family trust), which preserves the family's assets.

During your lifetime, as the sole trustee, you retain control of the trust and avoid trust management fees. You can alter the document or revoke it at any time. Assets in a living trust can be distributed right away, at any time, if desired. After your death, the trust continues to exist and to serve the purpose for which it was established, as if nothing has happened—except that it is now irrevocable, since the person with the power to revoke it has died. A successor trustee manages or distributes the assets according to your instructions as outlined in the trust document.

You can also set up a trust if you become disabled, with a trustee whom you appoint. However, remember that avoiding probate by appointing a trustee means you usually forfeit court supervision of your estate. Be cautious about whom—you appoint as a trustee. You can, however, remove a trustee if you wish.

What is the problem with probate? If an inheritance is handled by a probate court, the costs are higher, and the decisions are made by "strangers" rather than family members. Estates go into probate when there is no will or when there are disputes over the will, even if the will is valid.

A living trust can be especially helpful in the following cases:

- If you live in a state with costly and lengthy probate procedures. The procedure can take anywhere from a few months to a year in some states and consume between 3 and 5 percent (and sometimes 10 percent) of your estate.

- When your estate is large or complex and/or holds several liquid assets, such as real estate holdings in more than one state.

- If you fear a battle over the provisions of your will. Living trusts are more difficult to contest, with the exception of the statutory rights of a spouse and children.

- If you want privacy for your heirs. While assets passing through probate become public record, living trusts are much more private.

Distribution of assets within the living trust cannot be challenged in a probate court, but they are subject to claim by creditors. In a revocable living trust, you do not give up control over these assets, hence you have full access to the trust; because of this, you do not have asset protection against potential frivolous lawsuits. Assets held in this type of trust remain in your taxable estate, and you are taxed on income that comes from these assets.

Irrevocable Trusts

An irrevocable trust, on the other hand, separates the assets from one's estate (hence it offers asset protection) and reduces estate taxes. But it means that you must sacrifice control of the assets while you are alive, and you cannot make any changes by amending the trust. Instead, an independent trustee manages the assets for the benefit of all trust beneficiaries.

Whichever type of trust or other vehicle you choose, it will protect your hard-earned assets. To protect your residence (from personal or professional lawsuits), an irrevocable trust can be in the form of a Qualified Personal Residence Trust (QPRT).

A detailed discussion on the various types of irrevocable trusts is beyond the scope of this book. Please seek the counsel of your financial attorney or advisor for guidance suitable to your particular situation.

Family Limited Partnership (FLP)

The other crucial aspect of estate planning is asset protection, perhaps through a family-owned limited liability partnership. A family limited partnership (FLP) is generally owned by the husband, wife, and children. The FLP may own your share in a professional corporation, business, or other investments.

An FLP is a limited partnership formed to hold the family business or investments on a long-term basis, with the idea that the parents will make equal gifts of their limited partnership interests to their children during their lifetime. Because the limited partnership interests are illiquid and may not control decision making, so the theory goes, they should be subject to substantial discounts for federal gift tax and estate tax purposes. This means that if the FLP, for example, has assets worth $100,000, one may argue after discounts for lack of liquidity (no readily available market) and lack of control (passive investor without much say) that 100 percent of the FLP is worth only $70,000.

The FLP has certain unique attributes that are beneficial for both asset protection and estate planning. Regarding asset protection, the law (in certain states) limits a creditor to foreclosure on a partner's interest in an

FLP. The creditor who demands money from an FLP partner may have only a "charging order," which is not useful for most creditors. However, in some states, a creditor is permitted to "foreclose" on a partnership interest. A "foreclosure," a seizure of the debtor's interest, is a powerful weapon for the creditor (plaintiff). Every plan that involves an FLP must therefore protect ownership interests with a trust designed for that purpose. The highest level of asset protection uses an asset-protection trust to hold the limited partnership interest in the FLP.

The limited partners of an FLP have the right to enjoy the income upon distribution. However, the general partner cannot use the assets of this FLP like his or her personal checkbook. The FLP is a distinct entity, separate from the general partner personally, and this distinction should be respected. Otherwise the benefits of forming the FLP can be lost.

My family, with the help of an attorney, formed a family limited partnership (FLP). Each child (irrespective of gender) owns an equal share as a limited partner, and my wife and I each own a small percentage while also serving as general partner. Over time, we have gifted a portion of our investments to this FLP. Each child has a capital account that is used to pay for his or her education and major expenses (such as housing, maintenance, marriage, car, computers, etc.)

This has worked out even better than we had anticipated. For example, the income of the partnership (which is mostly owned by the children) is allocated to each limited partner, who is paying taxes at a much lower rate than the parents. Since their capital accounts are defined, each child has the incentive to spend less and to save for the future, for instance, by graduating early to save tuition fees. Delaying withdrawals keeps money invested and growing for everyone. If one partner needs more funds, the others are willing to let him or her withdraw them, because that is what family is all about: helping each other. For example, the partners can agree to let the oldest one withdraw more funds to buy a home, and later, when enough funds are available, another child can buy a home, and so on.

Other Financial Vehicles

Other financial vehicles can be used to build or protect your wealth. A private insurance company can be established offshore and registered with the Internal Revenue Service (IRS) under Section 501(c)(15). The IRS exempts some US income and capital gains, and these can be used to write insurance policies (for example, for a medical practice). Assets can be transferred using allowable annual gifts (in 2013, $14,000 per year per person) or using a lifetime Unified Credit (as of 2013, $5.25 million).

Afterword

It is my hope that the ideas in this book, applied correctly, will help you to manage your finances wisely. The book covers the financial and moral principles that can provide you with spiritual fulfillment and economic success. When you earn, save, invest, spend, and give based on the advice in this book, you can live debt free, with your assets protected, and be taxed fairly. Also, your family's needs will be taken care of both now and in the future.

The ideas in this book are based on my experience. Now you may benefit from them, or even improve upon them. If you have found the book useful, please pray for me and just like me make a donation to your favorite charity.

I'd like to end the book with the following hadith and a verse:

> The Prophet (pbuh) said: "O Allah! I seek refuge with You from worry and grief, I seek refuge with You from weakness and laziness, I seek refuge with You from cowardice and miserliness, and I seek refuge with You from being heavily in debt and from being overpowered by [other] men.

> "Our Lord! Accept [this service] from us: for thou are the All-Hearing, the All-Knowing." (Q. 2:127)

Resources

Sterling Management Group

Sterling Management Group, Inc. (SMG) offers business development and management consulting services to entrepreneurs in the United States and overseas. The firm offers an array of services engineered to help its clientele realize their goals and achieve the full potential from their business ventures. Some of SMG's services include (but are not limited to) the following:

- Asset management
- Accounting and financial management
- Business development services
- Raising Capital & other types of structured financing
- Investment management & advisory services
- Real Estate Acquisition, Development and Property Management (Residential and Commercial)
- Agro-Industrial & Food Processing advisory services (poultry, fruit juices, yeast, dairy, beef and sheep)

Sterling Management Group, Inc.
459 Herndon Parkway, Suite 22
Herndon, VA 20170 USA
Tel: (703) 471-6060
Fax: (703) 471-1211
www.sterlingmgmt.com

Sterling Charitable Gift Fund (a Donor-Advised Fund)

We encourage the spirit of helping the needy and the poor, and advancing the causes you believe in (such as education and healthcare).

The Sterling Charitable Gift Fund (SCGF) is a 501(c)(3) trust which assists with establishing an account in the donor's name and allows the donation of immediate funding of future charitable giving. Foundations serve the public interest now and in the future. The SCGF, provides a low-cost alternative to private "personal" foundations, and can help establish a waqf (endownment, a sadaqa jaria) at a lower cost and with greater tax benefits relative to a private foundation.

SMG also provides financial management, accounting and tax filing services for non-profit and charitable, private and public foundations (including endowment funds). SMG works with several attorneys who specialize in the legal aspects of establishing charitable entities, and obtaining tax-exempt status for them. For further information regarding the Sterling Charitable Gift Fund, please e-mail: gift@sterlingmgmt.com

International Institute of Islamic Thought (IIIT)

The International Institute of Islamic Thought (IIIT) is a cultural and intellectual foundation. IIIT was established in the United State of America at the beginning of the fifteenth Hijrah century (1401/1981) with the following objectives:

- Elucidating the principals of Islam and relating them to relevant issues of contemporary thought.

- Regaining the intellectual, cultural, and civilizational identity of the Ummah through the Islamization of the humanities and social sciences.

- To rectify the methodology of contemporary Islamic thought in order to enable it to resume its contribution to the progress of human civilization and give it meaning and direction in line with the values and objectives of Islam.

The Institute seeks to achieve its objectives by:

- Holding specialized academic conferences and seminars.

- Supporting and publishing selected works of scholars and researchers in universities and academic research centers in the Muslim world and the West.

- Helping university students work on issues of Islamic thought and the Islamization of Knowledge.

IIIT has a number of overseas offices, affiliates and academic advisors for the purpose of coordinating and promoting its research and academic activities. The Institute has also entered into joint academic agreements with several universities and research centers.

International Institute of Islamic Thought
500 Grove Street
Herndon, VA 22070-4705, USA
Tel: (703) 471-1133
Fax: (703) 471-3922
Email: iiit@iiit.org
www.iiit.org

The Fairfax Institute (TFI)

The Fairfax Institute (TFI) is a Northern Virginia based center of knowledge committed to continuing education and lifelong learning. TFI offers an instructional program to help students, academicians, lifelong learners, and concerned citizens, as well as professionals in government, policymaking, business, and information analysis, to enhance their skills through a better understanding of the laws, traditions and culture of Islam and the Muslim world.

Its vision is to become a platform for continuing education and lifelong learning through an open exchange of ideas and information that enhance religious and spiritual understanding, develop performance skills, achieve professional growth, and enrich people's intellectual lives

The Fairfax Institute
500 Grove Street, 2nd Floor
Herndon, VA 20170 USA
Tel: (703) 478-9222
Fax: (703) 935-1459
Email: admissions@fairfaxi.net
www.fairfaxi.net

The Foundation for Appropriate and Immediate Temporary Help (FAITH)

The Foundation for Appropriate and Immediate Temporary Help (FAITH). FAITH is located in Herndon, Virginia, and was established in 1999. FAITH is a recognized section 501(c) 3 tax exempt corporation.

FAITH's vision is to strengthen the community by helping individuals and families lead dignified and harmonious lives. Its mission is to provide humanitarian aid to individuals and families in need who are living in Northern Virginia. FAITH serves people of all faiths and ethnicities, and the majority of FAITH clients are from Muslim-based cultures. In addition to providing humanitarian aid to the local community, for the last ten years FAITH has led a pioneering effort to help women who have been the victims of domestic violence.

FAITH provides a variety of services to the Northern Virginia community, which includes direct services to domestic violence victims and their children through the following programs:

- Safe and Peaceful Families Program
- Food Pantry
- Thrift Store
- Self-Sufficiency Program

FAITH Social Services
795 Center Street, Unit 2
Herndon, VA 20170-4685
Tel: (571) 323-2198
Web: www.faithus.org

Amana Mutual Fund

Amana Mutual Funds Trust (Ticker symbols: AMANX, AMAGX, and AM-DWX), headquartered in Bellingham, Washington, USA, is a mutual fund company offering investment products consistent with Islamic banking principles.

The Amana Income Fund, founded by Unified Management Corporation, Indianapolis, IN, in 1986, was the Trust's first fund. The Amana Growth Fund was created in 1994. The Amana Developing World Fund was created in 2009. All three funds are managed according to Islamic principles.

Traditional mutual funds are off-limits to Muslims, because they typically contain securities that are forbidden by Shari'ah law. Accordingly, the Amana Funds are managed under strict guidelines to comply with Islamic principles. Examples of forbidden (haram) investments are companies that:

- Produce or sell alcohol, tobacco or pornography
- Process or sell pork products
- Generate revenue from gambling or interest (riba)
- Maintain a debt ratio of greater than one-third of assets

These funds were created and are still managed under the value investment style. Mr. Nicholas Kaiser has been portfolio manager of the funds since 1990. Saturna Capital advises Amana on its funds and investments.

Amana Mutual Funds Trust
P.O. Box N
Bellingham, WA 98227
www.amanafunds.com

Saturna Capital Headquarters
1300 N. State St.
Bellingham, WA 98225
Ph: (360) 734-9900
Fx: (360) 734-0755

University Bank

University Bank is a community bank based in Ann Arbor, Michigan, USA, serving the diverse needs of all consumers. University Bank is proud to have formed University Islamic Financial Corporation, the first Islamic Banking subsidiary run entirely on Shari'ah principles. UIFC serves the needs of the Muslim community by offering Shari'ah-compliant deposit accounts through University Bank and Mortgage Alternative (MALT™) products.

University Bank's subsidiary, University Insurance & Investment Services, makes Shari'ah-compliant Mutual Funds available to its customers. The bank's goals are to provide more Shari'ah-compliant products in order to be a single point of contact for all of their customers financial services needs.

University Bank
Headquarters:
2015 Washtenaw Avenue
Ann Arbor MI 48104
www.university-bank.com

Toll Free: 1-800-916-UIFC
Fax: 1-800-215-5207 / 734-822-0016

University Islamic Financial
Headquarters:
30500 Northwestern Highway, Suite #315
Farmington Hills, MI 48334
wwww.universityislamicfinancial.com

Telephone: (248) 254-7054
Fax: (248) 254-7055

Notes

Introduction

1. Irfan Ul Haq, *Economic Doctrines of Islam: A Study in the Doctrines of Islam and Their Implications for Poverty, Employment and Economic Growth* (Herndon, VA: International Institute of Islamic Thought, 1996), p. 245.
2. Gary A. Moore, *Faithful Finances 101: From Poverty of Fear and Greed to the Riches of Spiritual Investing* (Radnor, PA: Templeton Press, 2005), pp. 3–4.
3. Ibid., p. 32.
4. Ibid., p. 2.
5. Ibid., p. 44.
6. Ibid., p. 15.
7. Shaykh Yusuf Talal DeLorenzo, "Preface" in Virginia Morris and Brian D. Ingram, *Guide to Understanding Islamic Investing in Accordance with Islamic Shariah* (New York: Lightbulb Press, 2001), p. 3.
8. Lynnette Khalfani, *Zero Debt—The Ultimate Guide to Financial Freedom* (New Jersey: Advantage World Press, 2004), p. 8.
9. *Sahih al Bukhari* 2:292, cited in Irfan Ul Haq, *Economic Doctrines of Islam*, p. 114.
10. Also see Suze Orman, *The 9 Steps to Financial Freedom: Practical and Spiritual Steps so You Can Stop Worrying* (New York: Three Rivers Press, 2006).
11. Hadith of the Prophet Muhammad, reported by Abu Daoud.
12. Hadith, reported by al-Nisai and al-Hakim.
13. Hadith, reported by al-Bukhari.
14. Ul Haq, *Economic Doctrines of Islam*, p. 114.
15. Hadith, reported by Muslim.
16. Hadith, reported by al-Bukhari.
17. Portions of this chapter reference Yusuf al-Qaradawi, *Halal and Haram in Islam* (Indianapolis, IN: American Trust Publications, 1987), pp. 268–269, concerning the Prophet seeking refuge with God from debt.

18. Tarek El Diwany, ed., *Islamic Banking and Finance: What It Is and What It Could Be* (London: 1st Ethical Charitable Trust, U.K, 2010), p. 99.

19. M. Umer Chapra, *Towards a Just Monetary System: A Discussion of Money, Banking and Monetary Policy in the Light of Islamic Teachings* (London: The Islamic Foundation, 1995).

20. Morris and Ingram, *Guide to Understanding Islamic Investing*, p. 10.

21. Excerpted from Jerald F. Dirks, *The Abrahamic Faiths: Judaism, Christianity, and Islam: Similarities and Contrasts* (Beltsville, MD: Amana Publications, 2004), p. 29.

22. William W. Baker, *More In Common Than You Think: The Bridge Between Islam and Christianity.* (Crane, MO: Defender Publications, 1998).

23. "Oneness of Humanity," Los Angeles Chinese Learning Center, http://chinese-school.netfirms.com.

24. Muhammad Ali al-Hashimi, *The Ideal Muslim Society as Defined in the Qur'an and Sunnah* (Riyadh, Saudi Arabia: International Islamic Publishing House, 2010), p. 180.

25. al-Hashimi, *Ideal Muslim Society*, p. 180 (taken from Hadith as recorded by Bukhari and Muslim).

26. Ibid, p. 419.

27. Hadith narrated by Tabarâni and al-Bazzâr.

28. Ibrahim Abdul-Matin, *Green Deen: What Islam Teaches about Protecting the Planet* (San Francisco: Berrett-Koehler Publishers, 2010).

29. Remarks from a discussion I had with Joseph Montville, Chair, Center for World Religions, Diplomacy, and Conflict Resolution, George Mason University.

30. The *shahadah* is the first pillar of Islam. The shahadah is the declaration that "there is no god but Allah and Muhammad is the Prophet of God."

31. Fathi Osman, *Concepts of the Qur'an* (Los Angeles MVI Publications, 1997), p. 936.

32. Jessica Dulong, "The Imam of Bedford-Stuyvesant," *Aramco World*, May-June 2005.

Chapter 1

1. Adapted from Ul Haq, *Economic Doctrines of Islam*, pp. 92–95.

2. Sayings of Muhammad, cited in Siddiqi, *Economic Enterprise in Islam* (Lahore: Islamic Publications, 1972), pp. 12–13.

3. This section draws upon the pioneering work of Muhammad Nejatullah Siddiqi, *The Economic Enterprise in Islam* (Lahore: Islamic Publications, 1972).

4. Ul Haq, *Economic Doctrines of Islam*, pp.92–95.
5. *Saḥīḥ al Bukhārī* 3:349.
6. Siddiqi, *Economic Enterprise*, p.28.
7. Wayne Grudem, "How Business in Itself Can Glorify God," in Tetsunao Yamamori and Kenneth Eldred, *On Kingdom Business: Transforming Missions through Entrepreneurial Strategies* (Wheaton, IL: Crossway Books, 2003), p. 127.
8. Wayne Grudem, *Business for the Glory of God: The Bible's Teaching on the Moral Goodness of Business* (Wheaton, IL: Crossway Books, 2003), p.23.
9. Ibid., p. 37.
10. Muhammad Muhsin Khan, *Summarized Saḥīḥ al Bukhārī*, (Riyadh, Saudi Arabia: Darussalam, 1996), p. 17.
11. Ul Haq, *Economic Doctrines of Islam*, pp. 92–95.
12. The Fairfax Institute, located in Herndon, Virginia, offers a course on faith-based entrepreneurship. Those interested in pursuing and/or exploring entrepreneurship are encouraged to take this course. For more information on the course, contact the Institute at www.fairfaxi.net.
13. Stephen Owens, "Biblical Entrepreneurship: The Purpose of a Christian Entrepreneur,"http://ezinearticles.com/?Biblical-Entrepreneurship---The-Purpose-of-a-Christian-Entrepreneur&id=1222706

Chapter 2

1. Ul Haq, *Economic Doctrines of Islam*, pp.92–95.
2. Ibid., p.24.
3. Dwight Nichols, *God's Plans for Your Finances* (New Kensington, PA: Whitaker House, 1998), p. 55.
4. Scottrade, *2011 American Retirement Survey* (St. Louis: Scottrade, 2011).
5. Moore, *Faithful Finances 101*, p. 44.
6. Omar Clark Fisher, *Islamic Wealth Guide: Guide to Wealth Building, Risk Management and Wealth Distribution in Accordance with Islamic Shariah* (Oakton, VA: Self-published, 2007), p. 42.
7. Reported by al-Nisai and al-Hakim.
8. Hadith reported by al-Bukhari.
9. From website: http://www.fbcsomerset.com/dfree.php.
10. Deforest Soaries, "Debt-free Living is the Key to Power," CNN wesbite, November 14, 2010, http://www.cnn.com/2010/OPINION/10/17/inam.soaries.dfree.pulpit/index.html.
11. Gary Moore, *Faithful Finances 101*, p. 42.

12. Michelle Singletary, *7 Money Mantras for a Richer Life: How to Live Well with the Money You Have* (New York: Random House, 2003).

13. Starbuck Investor Relations, Financial Release (Seattle: Starbucks Coffee Company, 2011).

14. CNBC 1-hour interview, http://richmanramblings.blogspotcom/2008/11/warren-buffet.html.

15. Warren Buffet and Lawerence Cunningham, *The Essays of Warren Buffet: Lessons for Corporate America* (New York: The Cunningham Group, 2008).

Chapter 3

1. Ul Haq, *Economic Doctrines of Islam*, p. 158.

2. Ibid.

3. "Warren Buffett, The Billionaire Next Door," May 7, 2007, http://www.cnbc.com/id/17595710.

4. Statements made in this chapter are for educational purposes only, and are not be taken as investment advice. Please consult your financial advisors before implementing any of these suggestions.

5. Michael Mauboussin, "Why Smart People Make Dumb Decisions," *The Futurist* 44:2 (March 6, 2010).

6. Virginia Morris, *A Muslim's Guide to Investing and Personal Finance* (New York: Lighthouse Press, 2009).

7. Ramit Sethi, *I Will Teach You to Be Rich* (New York: Workman, 2009). In my opinion, Sethi's book is a fine read. The section on house buying begins on p. 250.

8. Robert Shiller, quoted in ibid., p. 253.

9. These charts are available at www.econ.yale.edu/~shiller/data/Fig2-1.xlsSimilar.

10. Sethi, *I Will Teach You*, p. 253.

11. Morningstar: www.morningstar.com; Lipper: www.lipperweb.com

12. Ruthie Ackerman, "God's My Investment Advisor: Faith-Based Funds Doing Well," *American Banker*, December 21, 2009, p. 6.

13. Jay Peroni, cited in ibid., p.15.

14. Daren Fonda, "Faith & Finance," *Smart Money*, January 2010, pp. 62–67.

15. Mufti Muhammad Taqi Usmani, "Looking for New Steps in Islamic Finance," www.muftitaqiusmani.com.

16. Office of the Comptroller of the Currency Interpretive Letters 806 and 867 (issued December 1997 and November 1999, respectively) provide

exceptions to the National Bank Act of 1864, which states that banks cannot hold legal title or possess any real estate to secure any debt to it for a period exceeding five years. We expect permission to be granted soon on *itisna'a* contracts.

17. Ibrahim Warde, quoted in Elizabeth Ferruelo, "Why Socially Responsible Investing and Islamic Finance is on the Rise," Forbes.com, November 1, 2012, http://www.forbes.com/sites/ashoka/2012/11/01/why-there-is-high-growth-potential-in-the-nexus-between-socially-responsible-investing-and-islamic-finance/.

18. See the University Islamic Financial website: www.myuif.com. "FDIC insured" means that in the event of the bank's insolvency, insurance (on deposits up to $250,000 per account) is provided by the Federal Deposit Insurance Corporation.

Chapter 4

1. This UGMA account description is not comprehensive and you may want to do more research.

2. "Shared equity homeownership ensures that the homes remain affordable to lower income households on a long-term basis by restricting the appreciation that the owner can retain, preserving affordable housing in areas where rising prices are forcing lower income households out of the market. At the same time, by placing the owner within a community-based support system, such as a community land trust or limited equity cooperative, shared equity homeownership can mitigate the risks of homeownership, potentially increasing the benefits of homeownership both for the owner and the neighborhood in which she lives." Preface in John E. Davis, *Shared Equity Homeownership: The Changing Landscape of Resale-Restricted Owner-Occupied Housing* (Montclair, NJ: National Housing Institute, 2006). Available online at http://www.nhi.org/pdf/SharedEquityHome.pdf.

3. These mortgages to Fannie Mae and Freddie Mac have a financing limit of $417,000 per mortgage transaction. These numbers do tend to change over time; however, the general loan limits for 2013 remain unchanged from 2012 (e.g., $417,000 for a 1-unit property in the continental United States).

4. Amana has a system by which it can generate duplicate statements of accounts, one for the recipient and the other for the donor, to know how the investment is growing and to facilitate additional investments.

5. By withdrawing say, $12,000 each year, her retirement could last for more than for fifteen years.

6. Profit-sharing CDs are offered by certain institutions, such as University Bank (for more information, see www.University-Bank.com).

Chapter 5

1. *Sahih Al-Bukhari*, Volume 2, Hadith 524.
2. *Fiqh-us-Sunnnah*, Volume 3, Number 98.
3. Vijay Mahajan, *The Arab World Unbound* (San Francisco: Jossey-Bass, 2009), p. 108.
4. M. Umer Chapra, *Islam and the Economic Challenge* (Nairobi: The Islamic Foundation, 1982), p. 271.
5. Hadith reported by al-Tabarani
6. Author's note: To my understanding, the Qur'an does not distinguish between zakah and sadaqah. However, scholars have deemed zakah as mandatory, whereas voluntary contributions (more than zakah) are called sadaqah.
7. A dirham is an Arab coin, worth about 25 cents of buying power at the time of the Prophet.
8. Muhammad Ali al-Hashimi, *The Ideal Muslim Society as Defined in the Qur'an and Sunnah* (Riyad, Saudi Arabia: International Islamic Publishing House, 2010), p. 196.
9. Working draft opinion of Fiqh Council of North America, p. 16.
10. Benson Tesdahl, correspondence with the author, June 2010.
11. Yusuf al-Qardawi, *Fiqh az-Zakah: A Comparative Study* (London: Dar al-Taqwa Ltd., 1999). p. 353.
12. Mahmoud Abu Saud, *Contemporary Zakah* (Cincinnati, OH: Zakat and Research Foundation, 1988), p. 176.
13. Shaykh Safiur Rahman Al-Mubarakpuri, *Tafsir Ibn Kathir,* vol. 4, p. 349. (Riyad: Maktaba Dar-us-Salam, 2003).
14. Chapra, *Islam and the Economic Challenge*, pp. 272–273.
15. Abu-Saud, *Contemporary Zakah*, p. 72.
16. Hadith cited at http://www.amanafunds.com/retail/zakah/zakah2.shtml
17. Hadith reported by al-Tirmidhi.
18. Abu-Saud, M. *Contemporary Zakat*, p. 164.
19. Hadith, reported by al-Tirmidhi.
20. M. Siddiqi, "Zakah: Questions and Answers," *Islamic Horizons*, Nov.-Dec. 2000, p. 60.
21. Yusuf al-Qaradawi, *Fiqh az-Zakah* (London: Dar al-Taqwa, 1999), p. 333.
22. FAITH is a nonprofit organization providing humanitarian aid to the

needy in northern Virginia: the elderly, divorced, homeless, and victims of domestic violence.

23. Bukhari, Book 2 (vol. 24), hadith 500.

24. *Readings on Charity and Kindness in Islam* (Plainfield, IN: ISNA Development Foundation, 2002), p. 19.

25. "Giving While Living: Do Muslim Americans know why giving while living is more worthwhile?," M.Yaqub Mirza and Firas Barzinji, *Islamic Horizons* magazine, Nov/Dec 2003, p. 39.

26. Carnegie, Andrew, "The Gospel of Wealth, and other timely essays," (The De Vinne Press, New York, 1901), p. 10.

Chapter 6

1. Brian D. Ingram and Virginia B. Morris, *Guide to Understanding Islamic Investing* (New York: Lightbulb Press, 2001), p. 18.

2. Ibid., p. 19.

3. "Shaul Elnadav, "Estate Planning, Halacha and the Jewish Law of Inheritance," http://jlperspectives.org/2010/01/15/estate-planning-halacha-and-the-jewish-law-of-inheritance/.

4. Geoffrey St. Marie, "Christian Inheritance Law," www.ehow.com /facts_6831123/Christian-inheritance-law.html.

5. Chapra, *Islam and the Economic Challenge*, p. 275.

6. Ahmad, al-Tirmidhi, ibn Majah, and Abu Da'ud.

7. Ibid.

8. Mohammad Hashim Kamali, *Maqasid Al-Shariah: Ijtihad And Civilisational Renewal* (London: The International Institute of Islamic Thought, 2012), pp. 13-14.

9. Virginia Code § 64.1-13; § 64.1-16.

10. *Mahr* is treated as a liability within a will. Presentation made by Mazen Hashemi at IIIT, Herndon, VA, Summer 2011.

11. *Riyad-us-Saliheen*, Hadith: 353.

12. Hadith, reported by Al-Bukhari

13. Hadith, reported by Al-Bukhari.

14. Hadith, reported by Al-Tirmidhi.

15. Wills, trusts, asset protection, and estate planning are specialized and complex subjects, and providing complete, detailed information about each one is beyond the scope of this book. Before implementing any of these ideas, please consult an attorney who specializes in these matters.

16. Hadith, reported by Al-Tirmidhi.

17. Commentary by Abdullah Yusuf Ali—"Opinions differ whether the provision [of a year's maintenance, with residence], for a widow, is put aside by the share which the widow gets (one-eighth or one-fourth) as an heir (4:12). I do not think it is. The bequest (where made) takes effect as a charge on the property, but the widow can leave the house before the year is out, and presumably maintenance then ceases." Confirmed via email correspondence with author and Dr. Muzzamil Siddiqi, Chairman, Fiqh Council of North America, October 7, 2010.

18. This advice is taken from Herbert Nass, *The 101 Biggest Estate Planning Mistakes* (Hoboken, NJ: John Wiley and Sons, 2010), p. 42.

19. Probate is the process by which a probate Judge transfers assets to your heirs as provided in your will or, lacking a will, in accordance with state law.

Glossary

Abrahamic faiths—The monotheistic faiths that trace their common origin to Abraham or recognize a spiritual tradition identified with him. The three major Abrahamic religions are, in chronological order of founding, Judaism, Christianity, and Islam. All three conceive God to be a transcendent Creator-figure and the source of moral law, and their sacred narratives feature many of the same figures, histories, and places, although they often present these with different roles, perspectives, and meanings.

ahl al-kitab—"People of the book," that is, adherents to faiths that have a revealed scripture. The Qur'an mentions as people of the book: Jews, Sabians, Christians, and Muslims.

bay al-dayn—The Arabic term for trading debt. The majority of scholars consider the trading of debt similar to the trading of money. In general, this means that a debt can be transferred only at face value, not at market value, as many conventional bonds are traded.

charitable remainder trust (CRT)—A charitable giving vehicle in which assets (property or money) are donated to the CRT while the donor continues to use the property and/or receive income from it while living. Upon the donor's death or after a specified period the asset goes to the named charity.

da'wah—Propagation of faith; to invite to something. When this term is used in conjunction with Islam, it means "inviting to the Way of submission and surrender to Allah."

dollar-cost averaging—An investment of a fixed amount of money at regular intervals, usually each month. This results in the purchase of extra shares during market downturns and fewer shares during market upturns. Dollar-cost averaging is a way to avoid trying to time the market and usually results in a lower average cost per share.

donor-advised fund (DAF)—A charitable giving vehicle administered by a public charity and created for the purpose of managing charitable donations on behalf of an organization, family, or individual. A donor-advised fund is an easy-to-establish, low-cost, flexible vehicle for charitable giving and an alternative to direct giving or creating a private foundation. Donors enjoy administrative convenience, cost savings, and tax advantages by conducting their grant making through the fund without the pressure of time to make ultimate gifts.

education savings account (ESA)—An account into which one may deposit funds on a tax-deferred basis to pay for the education of the account holder. Formerly called an education IRA, the account's funds are invested in a portfolio, much like an IRA or other retirement account. If the funds are in fact used for education, withdrawals from the ESA are tax-exempt up to the total cost of education.

family foundation—A legal entity whose purpose is to fulfill the family's wishes and vision by giving charitable grants. A foundation gives monetary gifts for designated purposes, from its own funds and investment earnings to organizations engaged in religious, charitable, scientific, literary, or educational work, within the meaning of Internal Revenue Code 501(c)3.

family limited partnership (FLP)—A sophisticated financial planning technique that, when implemented properly, enables a family to hold and manage its wealth, including the family business, with several generations of family members as partners. It may also provide asset protection.

faqih—Islamic legal expert; Islamic jurisprudence.

fard al-'ayn—An individual obligation.

fard al-kifayah—A communal obligation.

financial inventory—A master listing of all of one's personal assets and debts, including but not limited to cash, retirement accounts, life insurance policies, real estate, taxes owed, debt, credit card balances, and home equity loans.

fiqh—Islamic jurisprudence.

hadith—Narrative report of the sayings and actions of the Prophet Muhammad.

hadith qudsi—Sacred hadith; a hadith containing words of Allah narrated by the Prophet apart from the Qur'an.

hajj—The ritual pilgrimage to Mecca, Saudi Arabia. As the fifth pillar of Islam, the hajj is a religious duty that must be carried out at least once in the lifetime of every able-bodied Muslim who can afford to do so. One of the largest pilgrimages in the world (usually around 3 million people), the hajj is a demonstration of the solidarity of the Muslim people and of their submission to Allah.

halal—Islamically lawful, good, and permitted. An animal slaughtered Islamically, i.e., while calling, "In the name of Allah—Allah is great."

haram—Islamically unlawful or forbidden.

ijarah—Leasing. A contract in which the financier purchases an asset on behalf of the lessee and allows him or her to use it for a rental payment. The lessee may eventually opt to buy the assets at a previously agreed-upon price.

imam—Leader of a mosque/community; one who may lead prayer.

iman—Faith; religious belief or conviction in the fundamental doctrines of Islam.

interfaith movement—Cooperative and constructive interaction among people of different religious traditions and/or spiritual or humanistic beliefs, at both the individual and institutional levels. Such interactions build on commonalities without focusing on differences.

investment portfolio—Consists of various investments, such as stocks, money market funds and cash equivalents, mutual funds, exchange-traded funds, and closed-end funds, selected on the basis of an investor's short-term or long-term investment goals. Generally, portfolios are held directly by investors and/or managed by financial professionals.

Islam—Submission or surrender to the will of God.

istisna'a—A contract of exchange with deferred delivery applied to specified made-to-order items. Istisna'a differs from ijarah in that the manufacturer must procure his own raw materials.

jurist—Islamic scholar trained in Islamic law.

kufr—Rejection of God's teachings; disbelief.

mahr—Bridal money given by the husband to his wife at the time of marriage; dower.

mudarabah—A contract under which the supplier of capital and the entrepreneur (general partner) share the profits according to an agreed-upon profit loss sharing (PLS) ratio.

murabahah—A cost-plus-profit margin contract whereby the financier purchases an asset on behalf of an entrepreneur and sells it (usually at a higher price) to the entrepreneur at a predetermined price, paid over time.

musharakah—A partnership contract between two or more parties, each of which contributes investment capital.

mutual fund—A pool of liquidity that an investment company places in various securities and/or derivatives with the goal of producing a certain return. Mutual funds may carry greater or lesser risk, depending on their particular investment goals. Mutual funds are actively managed by the company to maintain the investment goals. The company issues shares that represent a portion of ownership in each of the securities underlying the fund. Mutual funds are designed for investors who wish to take advantage of a highly diversified portfolio with a small amount of capital.

nisab—An amount a family needs to live a simple but decent life for one year; minimum amount of wealth or income subject to Zakah.

peace be upon him (pbuh)—Peace be upon him ("pbuh") is a phrase that Muslims often say after saying (or hearing) the name of one of the Abrahamic prophets, including Muhammad.

Prophet Muhammad—Muslims believe the Prophet Muhammad was the last and the final messenger of God, who received the Qur'an, the final book.

qard al-hasan—Benevolence loan; a zero-return loan (a negative investment). A great vehicle for community development, this is not a profit-making transaction; it is a social service vehicle that provides an interest-free loan to individual or institution.

Qur'an—The central religious text of Islam, which Muslims consider the verbatim word of God. The Qur'an is composed of verses (*ayah*) that make up 114 chapters (*surah*) of unequal length, classified as either Meccan or Medinan depending upon the place and time of their revelation. Muslims believe the Qur'an was verbally revealed through the angel Gabriel from God to Muhammad over a period of twenty-three years beginning in 610 CE, when Muhammad was forty, and concluding in 632 CE, the year of his death.

rainy day fund—An emergency fund equal to approximately six months' expenses.

riba—Literally, increase, addition, expansion, or growth. In Shari'ah, riba refers to the interest or usury or "premium" that a borrower must pay to a lender along with the principal amount for postponing, deferring, or waiting for payment of a loan.

risk tolerance—The extent to which an investor is comfortable with the risk of losing money on an investment in exchange for a possibly higher return. An investor with a high risk tolerance is likely to invest in securities, such as stocks in startup companies, and is willing to accept the possibility that the value of his or her portfolio may decline, at least in the short-term. An investor with a low risk tolerance, on the other hand, tends to invest predominantly in stable stocks of well-established companies. One's risk tolerance is subjective and may vary according to age, needs, goals, and even personal dispositions.

Roth-IRA—An IRA (individual retirement account) that differs from most other tax-advantaged retirement plans in that the tax break is granted not when money is placed into the plan but on the money withdrawn from the plan during retirement.

sadaqah—Charity, the right of the poor; also used for zakah.

shahadah—The first pillar of Islam. Shahadah is the declaration that "there is no God but Allah and Prophet Muhammad is the Messenger of Allah."

Shari'ah—The moral code and religious law of Islam. Islamic law.

Shari'ah-compliant—A system following Islamic principles.

sunnah—The sayings and teachings of the Prophet Muhammad—his specific words, habits, practices, and silent approvals.

swt—An abbreviation for the expression of respect at the mention of God's name: subhanahu wa ta'ala, or "Glory to Him, the Exalted."

takaful—Pooled money for emergencies. Like a cooperative, this is a type of Islamic insurance in which members contribute money to a pooling system in order to guarantee each other against loss or damage. An alternative to conventional life and car insurance.

Talmud—The foundational document of Rabbinic Judaism. A vast compilation of Jewish oral law divided into six orders and sixty-three tractates.

Torah—Narrowly, the Five Books of Moses (Pentateuch); broadly, the whole body of Jewish learning and literature, written and oral.

tzedakah—Righteous giving. The obligation of Jews to give 10 percent of their net income to those in need.

ummah—Islamic community; the worldwide Muslim community.

umrah—A visit to Mecca, Saudi Arabia, performed by Muslims at any time of the year. It is sometimes called the mini pilgrimage or lesser pilgrimage, the hajj being the major pilgrimage and compulsory for every able-bodied Muslim who can afford it. The umrah is not compulsory but highly recommended.

waqf—An endowment, trust, or institution of ongoing charity. Principal to be held in trust; only the income can be used for a specified charitable or religious purpose.

zakah—Literally, to increase or cleanse. A fixed portion of one's wealth given to charity, generally to the poor and needy and others, as prescribed by the Qur'an and explained in hadith. An annual alms tithe of 2½ percent levied on wealth and distributed to the poor.

Bibliography

Abdul-Matin, Ibrahim. *Green Deen: What Islam Teaches about Protecting the Planet.* San Francisco: Berrett-Koehler Publishers, 2010.

Abu Saud, Mahmoud. *Contemporary Zakah.* Cincinnati, OH: Zakat and Research Foundation, 1988.

Ackerman, Ruthie. "God's My Investment Advisor: Faith-Based Funds Doing Well." *American Banker* (December 21, 2009).

Baker, William W. *More In Common Than You Think: The Bridge Between Islam and Christianity.* Crane, MO: Defendant Publications, 1998.

Buffet, Warren and Lawerence Cunningham. *The Essays of Warren Buffet: Lessons for Corporate America.* New York: The Cunningham Group, 2008.

Chapra, M. Umer. *Islam and the Economic Challenge.* Nairobi: The Islamic Foundation, 1982.

——. *Towards a Just Monetary System: A Discussion of Money, Banking and Monetary Policy in the Light of Islamic Teachings.* London: The Islamic Foundation, 1995.

Davis, John E. *Shared Equity Homeownership: The Changing Landscape of Resale-Restricted Owner-Occupied Housing.* Montclair, NJ: National Housing Institute, 2006.

Dirks, Jerald F. *The Abrahamic Faiths: Judaism, Christianity, and Islam: Similarities and Contrasts.* Beltsville, MD: Amana Publications, 2004.

DeLorenzo, Shaykh Yusuf Talal. "Preface" in Virginia Morris and Brian D. Ingram, *Guide to Understanding Islamic Investing in Accordance with Islamic Shariah.* New York: Lightbulb Press, 2001.

El Diwany, Tarek (ed.). *Islamic Banking and Finance: What It Is and What It Could Be.* London: 1st Ethical Charitable Trust, U.K, 2010.

DuLong, Jessica. "The Imam of Bedford-Stuyvesant." *Aramco World* (May-June 2005).

Elnadav, Shaul. "Estate Planning, Halacha and the Jewish Law of Inheritance." *Jewish Legal Perspectives* (January 15, 2010). http://jlperspectives.org/2010/01/15/estate-planning-halacha-and-the-jewish-law-of inheritance/

Fisher, Omar Clark. *Islamic Wealth Guide: Guide to Wealth Building, Risk Management and Wealth Distribution in Accordance with Islamic Shariah.* Oakton, VA: self published, 2007.

Ferruelo, Elizabeth. "Why Socially Responsible Investing and Islamic Finance is on the Rise." Forbes.com, November 1, 2012. http://www.forbes.com/sites/ashoka/2012/11/01/why-there-is-high-growth-potential-in-the-nexus-between-socially-responsible-investing-and-islamic-finance/.

Grudem, Wayne. *Business for the Glory of God: The Bible's Teaching on the Moral Goodness of Business.* Wheaton, IL: Crossway Books, 2003.

———. "How Business in Itself Can Glorify God." in Tetsunao Yamamori and Kenneth Eldred, *On Kingdom Business: Transforming Missions through Entrepreneurial Strategies.* Wheaton, IL: Crossway Books, 2003.

Haq, Irfan Ul. *Economic Doctrines of Islam: A Study in the Doctrines of Islam and Their Implications for Poverty, Employment and Economic Growth.* Herndon, Va.: International Institute of Islamic Thought, 1996.

al-Hashimi, Muhammad Ali. *The Ideal Muslim Society as Defined in the Qur'an and Sunnah.* Riyadh, Saudi Arabia: International Islamic Publishing House, 2010.

Kamali, Mohammad Hashim. *Maqasid Al-Shariah: Ijtihad and Civilizational Renewal.* London: The International Institute of Islamic Thought, 2012.

Khalfani, Lynnette. *Zero Debt—The Ultimate Guide to Financial Freedom.* South Orange, NJ: Advantage World Press, 2004).

Khan, Muhammad Muhsin. *Summarized Sahih al Bukkari.* Riyadh, Saudi Arabia: Darussalam 1996.

Mahajan, Vijay *The Arab World Unbound.* San Francisco: Jossey-Bass, 2009.

Mauboussin, Michael. "Why Smart People Make Dumb Decisions." *The Futurist* 44:2 (March 6, 2010).

Moore, Gary A. *Faithful Finances 101: From Poverty of Fear and Greed to the Riches of Spiritual Investing.* Radnor, PA: Templeton Press, 2005.

Morris, Virginia. *A Muslim's Guide to Investing and Personal Finance.* New York: Lighthouse Press, 2009.

Morris, Virginia and Brian D. Ingram. *Guide to Understanding Islamic Investing in Accordance with Islamic Shariah.* New York: Lightbulb Press, 2001.

Al-Mubarakpuri, Shaykh Safiur Rahman. *Tafsir Ibn Kathir,* vol. 4. Riyad: Maktaba Dar-us-Salam, 2003.

Nass, Herbert. *The 101 Biggest Estate Planning Mistakes.* Hoboken, NJ: John Wiley and Sons, 2010.

Nichols, Dwight. *God's Plans for Your Finances.* New Kensington, PA: Whitaker House, 1998.

Only for the Love of Allah by Night and by Day: Readings on Charity and Kindness in Islam. Plainfield, IN: ISNA Development Foundation, 2002.

Orman, Suze. *The 9 Steps to Financial Freedom: Practical and Spiritual Steps So You Can Stop Worrying*. New York: Three Rivers Press, 2006.

Osman, Fathi. *Concepts of the Quran*. Los Angeles: MVI Publications, 1997.

Owens, Stephen. "Biblical Entrepreneurship: The Purpose of a Christian Entrepreneur." *Ezine Articles*. http://ezinearticles. com/?Biblical-Entrepreneurship---The-Purpose-of-a-Christian-Entrepreneur&id=1222706

al-Qaradawi, Yusuf. *Halal and Haram in Islam*. Indianapolis, IN: American Trust Publications, 1987.

———. *Fiqh az-Zakah: A Comparative Study*. London: Dar al-Taqwa,1999.

Quilla, Oliver. "Warren Buffett, "The Billionaire Next Door." May 7, 2007. http://www.cnbc.com/id/17595710.

Scottrade. *2011 American Retirement Survey*. St. Louis: Scottrade, 2011.

Sethi, Ramit. *I Will Teach You to Be Rich*. New York: Workman, 2009.

Singletary, Michelle. *7 Money Mantras for a Richer Life: How to Live Well with the Money You Have*. New York: Random House, 2003.

Siddiqi, Muhammad N. *Economic Enterprise in Islam*. Lahore: Islamic Publications, 1972.

Soaries, Deforest. "Debt-free Living is the Key to Power." CNN article date 11/14/2010 http://www.cnn.com/2010/OPINION/10/17/inam.soaries. dfree.pulpit/index.html

St. Marie, Geoffrey. "Christian Inheritance Law." *EHow.Com*. www.ehow. com/facts_6831123/Christian-inheritance-law.html

Starbuck Investor Relations. *Financial Release*. Seattle, Washington: Starbucks Coffee Company, 2011.

Usmani, Mufti Muhammad Taqi. "Looking for New Steps in Islamic Finance." www.muftitaqiusmani.com.

About the Author

DR. M. YAQUB MIRZA is president and chief executive officer of Sterling Management Group, Inc. Sterling negotiates mergers, acquisitions, and sales of various-sized companies located in different parts of the world. Sterling and its affiliates operate in the United States, Canada, Chile, Egypt, Malaysia, Turkey, and Zimbabwe. In addition, Dr. Mirza has more than thirty years of experience in stock investments and portfolio management.

Dr. Mirza serves as the vice chairman of the board of trustees and chairman of the executive committee of Amana Mutual Funds, which is registered with the Securities and Exchange Commission. In addition, Dr. Mirza currently serves as chairman of Sterling Agricola, S.A., a Chilean company. He also serves on the boards of numerous other organizations, including several for-profit and not-for-profit, as well as academic institutions.

Dr. Mirza is a member of the Boards of Advisors for the College of Humanities and Social Sciences, George Mason University in Fairfax, Virginia, and the Board of Advisors, Byrd School of Business, Shenandoah University, Winchester, Virginia. He is a trustee on the George Mason University Foundation. He is also a member of the board's Investment and Endowment committee Shenandoah University.

He has received numerous awards and much recognition for his work in entrepreneurship and community service, including the 2002 Entrepreneur Award by the Islamic Chamber of Commerce and Industry (San Jose, California); 2006 Award Recipient—Byrd Distinguished Entrepreneur Speaker Series, Byrd School of Business at Shenandoah University; 2012 Recognition Award for Community Service by the American Muslim Alliance and 2013 Award from the Muslim American Coalition Council and Public Affairs Council. Most notably, Dr. Mirza was featured in an article on faith-based entrepreneurship, published in the 2010 spring edition of the *New England Journal of Entrepreneurship*.

Dr. Mirza holds a MSc from the University of Karachi (1969), a PhD in physics (1974) and an MA in teaching science (1975) from the University of Texas at Dallas.